THE PEOPLE

OF

JAMAICA

1655-1855

THE PEOPLE

OF

JAMAICA

1655-1855

By
David Dobson

CLEARFIELD

Printed for Clearfield Company by
Genealogical Publishing Company
Baltimore, Maryland
2019

ISBN 9780806358932

INTRODUCTION

In 1655 Oliver Cromwell, as part of his 'Western Design', invaded and captured Jamaica, which had been a Spanish colony. The Spanish heritage is evident in many of the island's place-names; however, most places in Jamaica were established and named by incoming settlers, mostly from England, with a minority from elsewhere in the British Isles. The economy was largely dependent on the production of sugar cane which resulted in slave labour largely brought from Africa. Jamaica was also a destination for prisoners of war, rebels, and criminals transported in chains to be sold as servants to the planters there. Many artisans emigrated from English ports, notably Bristol and London, as indentured servants to Jamaica, and were employed by merchants and planters who paid for their passage and maintenance for a few years before the servants were free to settle. The majority of white settlers in Jamaica clearly had their origins in the British Isles, however there were also French Huguenots, American Loyalists, and Jews there. While this source book may name a few Scots who appeared in my earlier book 'Scots in Jamaica, 1655-1855', [Baltimore, 2011], this new work is based on completely different sources.

This compilation is based on a range of primary sources, published and manuscript, located in libraries and archives in Jamaica, England, Wales, and Scotland.

David Dobson

Dundee, Scotland

2019

THE PEOPLE OF JAMAICA, 1655 TO 1855

ZANDER, Reverend CHRISTIAN, died in Jamaica in 1796.
[GM.89.1143]

REFERENCES

APCCol Acts Privy Council, Colonial, series

BM   = British Museum

Car   = Caribbeana, series

CSP = Calendar of State Papers, series

EMG = Edinburgh Medical Graduates, [Edinburgh, 1846]

GCA = Glasgow City Archives

GM   = Gentleman's Magazine, series

HMC = Historical Manuscript Commission

IRO = Island Record Office

JCTP = Journal of Committee Trade and Plantations

JHR = Jamaica Historical Review

LRO = Liverpool Record Office

NLW = National Library of Wales

NRS = National Records of Scotland

PCC = Prerogative Court of Canterbury

SPAWI State Papers, America, West Indies

THA = The National Archives, Kew

UL   = University of Leiden

THE PEOPLE OF JAMAICA, 1655 TO 1855

ABARBANEL, PHINEAS, a Jewish merchant in Jamaica, petitioned the Council for Trade and Plantations in London, on 30 August 1692. [JCTP]

ABICHAM, JOHN ANTHONY, from Jamaica, died in Uxbridge in 1790. [GM.60.478],

ABRAHAM, Mrs JANE, born 1655, died 30 January 1718. [Shaw Park gravestone, St Ann's, Jamaica]

ACKSON, THOMAS, a limner from London, died in Jamaica, probate, 1698, PCC

ADAMS, JOHN, from Stepney, London, died in Jamaica, administration, 1659, PCC

ADDISON, Reverend GEORGE AUGUSTUS, from Manchester, married Anna, second daughter of the late Charles Farquharson, in Clarendon, Jamaica, on 4 February 1851. [GM.ns35.545]

AERY, Dr THOMAS, died in Jamaica in 1790. [GM.60.1214]

AFFLECK, Miss, daughter of the late Dr Affleck, and sister of J. Affleck, a barrister in Spanish Town, Jamaica, died there on 8 November 1802. [GM.73.83]

AFFLICK, JAMES, born 1739, a carpenter from London, from London, bound via London aboard the Dawes for Jamaica in 1774. [TNA.T47.9/11]

AGUILAR, ABRAHAM, in London, son of Emanuel Aguilar in Jamaica, a deed re plantations in Jamaica, 1784. [Car.2.330]

AGUILAR, ISAAC, a merchant from Jamaica later in London, an indenture, 1812. [Car.2.367]

AGUILAR, JOSEPH, in London, son of Emanuel Aguilar in Jamaica, a deed re plantations in Jamaica, 1784. [Car.2.330]

AIKEN, ROGER, died in Jamaica in 1790. [GM.60.1053]

THE PEOPLE OF JAMAICA, 1655 TO 1855

AITKEN & Company, in Jamaica, a deed of factory with Paterson and Ainslie, 20 July 1802. [NRS.RD3.295.734]

ALDER, CHARLES, in Jamaica, a deed of attorney, 6 December 1788. [NRS.RD4.244.762]

ALDERSON, THOMAS, from Hertford, Jamaica, married Miss Boulby, daughter of Henry Boulby in Newcastle, in Denham, Norfolk, on 12 May 1789. [GM.59.467]

ALDRED, ANNA MARIA, born 1742, daughter of Daniel Broadbelt and his spouse Anna Maria, wife of Edward Alfred a surgeon, who died 21 December 1761. [St Catherine's gravestone, Jamaica]

ALEXANDER, HENRY, an American Loyalist, probably from South Carolina, who was granted land in St Elizabeth parish in 1782. [TNA]

ALEXANDER, JOHN, from St Olave, Southwark, London, died in Jamaica when bound for Carolina aboard the Nassau, probate, 1696, PCC

ALKIN, HENRY, from Uttoxeter, Staffordshire, died in Jamaica, admin. PCC

ALKIN, JAMES, from Uttoxeter, Staffordshire, died in Jamaica, admin. PCC

ALLAN, G., of the Colonial Bank in Kingston, Jamaica, married Charlotte, daughter of the late Reverend W. F. Ireland, in Cardiff, on 15 November 1836. [GM.ns7.92]

ALLEN, BENJAMIN, died in Jamaica in 1791. [GM.61.971]

ALLEN, SAMUEL, a planter in St David's, Jamaica, probate, 1698, PCC

ALLEN, SAMUEL, a pilot, died in Port Royal, Jamaica, in 1793. [GM.63.1152]

THE PEOPLE OF JAMAICA, 1655 TO 1855

ALLEN, WILLIAM, a labourer from London, died in Jamaica, probate, 1682, PCC

ALLEY, W. H., a former Captain of the 4th Regiment, a Special Justice, died in Jamaica on 24 August 1837. [GM.nsS9.222]

ALLIN, Miss, daughter of Jacob Allin in Jamaica, married Samuel Whitcomb, in Lillington, Dorset, on 27 May 1742. [GM.19.236]

ALPRESS, SAMUEL, of His Majesty's Council in Jamaica, died there in 1784. [GM.53.797]

ALVARENGA, ISAAC D'ACOSTA, probate, 1755.

ANDREISS, BARNARD, born 1640, Custos Rotulorum of St Elizabeth's, Jamaica, died 23 May 1719. [Lacovia Estate gravestone]

ANDREWS, J. D., of Port Antonio, married Eliza Panton, in Manchineal, Jamaica, in 1800. [GM.70.1283]

ANDREWS, WILLIAM, born 1793, late in Jamaica, died in Kensington, London, on 27 November 1854. [GM.ns43.109]

ANNESLEY, WILLIAM GROVE, Captain of the 6th Regiment, son of the late General A. G. Annesley of County Cork, married Eliza, second daughter of John Taylor of Good Hope Estate, Jamaica, in St Michael's, Port Royal, Jamaica, on 8 March 1866. [GM.ns3/1.737]

ANSTEY, SOPHIA CAROLINE, third daughter of William Jekyll Anstey, late Post-master General of Jamaica, married William Castle Smith, MD, in Bideford, London, on 19 November 1846. [GM.ns27.195]

ANTHONY, GEORGE, nephew of Lieutenant General Sir John Wilson, died in Jamaica on 15 November 1844. [GM.ns23.222]

ANTROBUS, Captain, from Bristol, died in Jamaica on 10 February 1811. [GM.81.492]

3

THE PEOPLE OF JAMAICA, 1655 TO 1855

ANYAN, SAMUEL, from Stepney, London, a mariner, died in Jamaica, probate, 1696, PCC

ARCEDECKNE, ANDREW, in Jamaica, died on 1 October 1783. [GM.33.518]; born in Ireland, a barrister at law. [St Catherine's gravestone, Jamaica]

ARCHBOULD, HENRY, in Port Royal, 1664. [BM.Add.ms12423/99]

ARCHER, EDWARD, born 1798, son of the late W. Archer, died in Jamaica on 18 June 1818. [GM.88.373]

ARCHER, FRANCIS, born 1789, died 8 February 1824. [St Catherine's gravestone, Jamaica]

ARCHER, GEORGE, of Spring Mount, and Greenfield, Jamaica, a journal, 1828 – 1841. [BM. Newcastle. Add.33294]

ARMOUR, Mrs ELIZABETH, born 1792, died 27 October 1827. [Kingston gravestone, Jamaica]

ARNNO, JOHN, an able seaman aboard the frigate Gloucester at Jamaica, probate, 1656, PCC

ARNOLD, WILLIAM, MD, born 1791, died in Kingston, Jamaica, on 20 June 1848. [GM.ns30.446]

ARPENASUS, ..., in Port Royal, 1677. [IRO.Deeds.viii.87]

ASHLEY, JOSEPH BISCOE, born 1814, son of John Ashley of Ashley Hall, Jamaica, died in Gloucester, on 15 May 1837. [GM.ns8.100]

ASKEW, LEONARD, settled in America for 30 years, a Loyalist soldier in 1776, moved to Jamaica by 1783, dead by 1789. [TNA.A12.51.82 etc]

ASSAM, WILLIAM, born 1685, died 1730, his wife Mary, born 1658, died 1734. [St Catherine's gravestone, Jamaica]

THE PEOPLE OF JAMAICA, 1655 TO 1855

ATHERTON, WILLIAM, in Preston, Lancashire, formerly of Trelawney and Kingston, Jamaica, letters, 1783-1802. [Lancashire Record Office, DDDPr.32/1-4]

ATKINSON, CHARLES, born 1647, died 20 November 1678. [St Catherine's gravestone, Jamaica]

ATKINSON, GEORGE, the Secretary of Jamaica, married Susannah Mackenzie Dunkley, in Clarendon, Jamaica, in 1794. [GM.64.956]

ATKINSON, JOHN, born 1655, died 10 November 1683. [St Catherine's gravestone, Jamaica]

ATKINSON, JOHN, was buried on 11 February 1798. [Kingston gravestone, Jamaica]

AUSTIN, THOMAS, born 1754, an attorney, with his sisters Martha, born 1756, and Ann, born 1757, from Dorset, bound via London aboard the Northampton for Jamaica in 1774. [TNA.T47.9/11]

AVIS, ROBERT, born 1729, a gentleman from London, bound aboard the Woodley bound via London for Jamaica in 1774. [TNA.T47.9/11]

AXTELL, WILLIAM, born 1720 in Jamaica, a Loyalist from New York, died in Chertsea, Sussex, on 2 September 1795. [GM.65.794]

AYLMER, Colonel WHITGIFT, born 1640, died 20 July 1707, his wife Joyce, born 1650, died 18 September 1707. [St John's gravestone, Jamaica]

AYREY, CHARLIANNA, born 1814, died 17 February 1839, also Elizabeth Ayrey, born 1823, died 27 March 1839. [Shekles Estate, Clarendon, gravestone, Jamaica]

BACHE, SAMUEL, an armiger, formerly in Port Royal, Jamaica, later in London, died in Clapham, Surrey, probate, 1687, PCC

BACH and HUDSON, merchants in Bird's Alley, Port Royal, 1679. [IRO. Deeds.vi.156]

THE PEOPLE OF JAMAICA, 1655 TO 1855

BACON, WILLIAM, a merchant in Kingston, Jamaica, a copy will, 1782. [Norfolk Record Office, ms 17258]

BAGNELL, JOHN, fought at the Battle of Sedgemoor in Somerset, on 6 July 1685 against the forces of King James II, captured and transported from Portland Road aboard the Jamaican Merchant of London, master Charles Gardiner, bound for Jamaica in 1685.

BALDWIN, WILLIAM, born 1701, died 17 July 1755, husband of Mary, born 1692, died 12 April 1760. [St Catherine's gravestone, Jamaica]

BAILEY, AGNES, born 1724, died 1 May 1749. [Kingston gravestone, Jamaica]

BAILEY, WILLIAM, born 1787, late of Jamaica and Horton Lodge, Buckinghamshire, died 16 September 1819. [GM.89.379]

BAILLIE, JAMES, a surveyor, died in Claredon, Jamaica, on 12 October 1789. [GM.60.179]

BAILLIE, SAMUEL CROOKSHANKS, died in Jamaica in 1790. [GM.60.476]

BAILEY, Mr, died aboard the Jamaica on passage to Jamaica on 10 May 1798. [GM.68.903]

BAINBRIDGE, Miss, daughter of the late Thomas Bainbridge in Jamaica, married George Wyatt in Hatton Garden, London, on 25 July 1795. [GM.66.614]

BAIRD, ADAM, died in Jamaica in 1790. [GM.60.1214]

BAKER, EDWARD, born 5 September 1779, a midshipman in the Royal Navy, died 21 April 1796. [Kingston gravestone, Jamaica]

BAKER, RICHARD, a mariner from Wapping, London, died in Jamaica, probate, 1694, PCC

BAKER, Mrs, widow of John Proculus Baker in Jamaica, died in Exeter on 3 March 1800. [GM.70.389]

THE PEOPLE OF JAMAICA, 1655 TO 1855

BALL, JOHN, a Lieutenant of the Royal Navy, of Vere parish, Withy Wood, Jamaica, probate, 1698, PCC

BALTHROPP, Mrs HESTER, born 1611, died 3 October 1679, daughter of Sir John Colte, and wife of Richard Balthropp of Gray's Inn Estate, parents of Richard, John, Alberticus Gentills, Margaret, Ann, and Hester. [St John's gravestone, Jamaica]

BANNISTER Major General JAMES, born 1624, late Governor of Surinam, died 10 November 1674. [St Catherine's gravestone, Jamaica]

BANNISTER, MARY, daughter of James Bannister, born 1659, died 2 January 1677, wife of Samuel Lewis. [St Catherine's gravestone, Jamaica]

BANNISTER, THOMAS, a clerk from London, bound via London aboard the Dawes for Jamaica in 1774. [TNA.T47.9/11]

BARAK, ISAAC MOSES, a Jewish merchant in Jamaica, petitioned the Council for Trade and Plantations in London, on 30 August 1692. [JCTP]

BARCLAY, JAMES, a planter of 30 acres in St Andrew's parish, Jamaica, in 1754. [TNA.CO137/28/171-196]

BARHAM, HENRY, born 1670, died 1726. [St Catherine's gravestone, Jamaica]

BARKER, WILLIAM, born 1744, a blacksmith from London, bound via London aboard the Mars for Jamaica in 1774. [TNA.T47.9/11]

BARNES, HANNAH, born 1766, widow of Joseph Barnes, Judge of the Supreme Court of Jamaica, and former Mayor of Kingston, Jamaica, died in Bristol on 13 January 1841. [GM.ns15.331]

BARNETT, CHARLES, youngest son of the late H. Barnett in Cobrey, Herefordshire, died in Jamaica on 17 September 1853. [GM.ns40.649]

BARNETT, FRANCES, from Jamaica, married Edward Woolery in Isleworth on 18 September 1760. [GM.30.490]

BARRE, CHARLES, tavern-keeper, and wife Mary, in Port Royal, 1689. [IRO.Deeds.xxi.31]

BARTLETT, HENRY, of St Margaret, Westminster, died in Jamaica, admin. 1656, PCC

BARNETT, HUGH, from Jamaica, died in Kingsdown on 6 May 1823. [GM.93.477]

BARNETT, MARY ANN, widow of Hugh Barnett of Sportsmanhall Estate, Jamaica, died in Barnstaple, Devon, on 28 October 1846. [GM.ns26.665]

BARNETT, SAMUEL, died in Jamaica in 1800. [GM.70.905]

BARNET, WILLIAM, of Jamaica, married Miss Wooling in Jamaica on 11 September 1764. [GM.34.497]

BARNETT, Miss, daughter of W. Barnett in Jamaica, married Reverend J. Smith, chaplain to the House of Commons, on 9 August 1803. [GM.73.788]

BARNETT, Mr, Chief Justice, died in St Anne's, Jamaica, in 1781. [GM.51.394]

BARNSDALE, BENNALL, born 1803, a printer and publisher of 'The Baptist Herald and Friend of Africa', died in Falmouth, Jamaica, on 13 September 1841. [GM.ns17.118]

BARR, ROBERT, in Jamaica, son of Peter Barr in Hutchesontown, Glasgow, a letter, 1846. [GCA.GB23D1710]

BARRETT, EDWARD, a merchant in Jamaica, 1670. [IRO.Deeds.iii.46]

THE PEOPLE OF JAMAICA, 1655 TO 1855

BARRETT, GEORGE GOODIN, a judge, politician and militia officer, died at Cambridge Pen, St Thomas in the East, Jamaica, in October 1795. [GM.65.1112]

BARRITT, HEARCEY, born 1650, died 5 March 1726. [St Catherine's gravestone, Jamaica]

BARRETT, LUCAS, F.G.S., F.L.S., Director of the West Indian Geological Survey, was drowned near Port Royal, Jamaica, on 19 December 1862. [St Andrew's gravestone, Jamaica]

BARRETT, S., from Jamaica, married Margaret Gillies Storey, daughter of Robert Storey, in Arcot, Northumberland, on 7 March 1812. [GM.82.288]

BARRETT, S. M., from Carleton Hall, Yorkshire, died at Cinnamon Hill, Jamaica, on 23 December 1837. [GM.ns9.334]

BARRITT, THOMAS, his first wife Susanna, born 1692, died 14 January 1728, parents of Thomas, Thomas, Susanna and Hearcey, his second wife Elizabeth, born 1693, died 1740. [St Catherine's gravestone, Jamaica]

BARRETT, Miss, daughter of Wisdom Barrett in Jamaica, married James Trant from Montserrat, in London i1798. [GM.68.1147]

BARRINGTON, FRANCIS, in Jamaica, a letter, 1657. [Bodleian Library, Rawlinson, A53]; in Jamaica, letters, 1655-1659. [BM, Egerton.2648]

BARROW, FRANCIS, born 1824, tenth son of John Barrow in Wedmore, Somerset, died in Jamaica in 1842. [GM.ns18.335]

BARROW, T., settled in Jamaica around 1682, the Attorney General of Jamaica before 1706. [APCCol.177]

BARTLET, HENRY, from Westminster, died in Jamaica, admin., 1656, PCC

THE PEOPLE OF JAMAICA, 1655 TO 1855

BARTON, JEREMIAH, a politician and militia officer, died in Old Harbour, Jamaica, on 4 November 1792. [GM.62.1220]

BARUK, MOSES, a Jew in Surinam petitioned to go to Jamaica in 1676. [SPAWI.1676.818.I]

BATEMAN, THOMAS GEORGE, born 1828, fourth son of Lieutenant Colonel Bateman, died in Kingston, Jamaica, on 1 December 1842. [GM.ns19.556]

BATHURST, JOHN, from Holburn, Middlesex, died in Jamaica, probate, 1694, PCC

BATTEN, Reverend CHARLES HAMILTON, born 1826, youngest son of the late Reverend Joseph Hallet Batten, Principal of Haileybury College, died in Kingston, Jamaica, on 14 November 1852. [GM.ns39.215]

BATTEY, RICHARD, born 1749, a gentleman from London, bound via London aboard the West Indian for Jamaica in 1774. [TNA.T47.9/11]; born 1743, died 10 April 1796. [St Catherine's gravestone, Jamaica]

BAYLEY, ALEXANDER, of Woodhall, St Dorothy, born 1772, died 14 July 1832. [St Catherine's gravestone, Jamaica]

BAYLEY, CHARLOTTE AUGUSTA, daughter of the late Alexander Bayley of Wood Hall, Jamaica, married Charles Lyall of Barbados, youngest son of John Lyell in Brighton, in Stapleton, Gloucestershire, on 21 August 1845. [GM.ns24.521]

BAYLEY, DIANA SARAH, daughter of Nathaniel Bayley in Jamaica, married Reverend Samuel Holworth of Craxall, Derby, in Cheshunt, on 8 April 1811. [GM.81.392]

BAYLEY, ROBERT SOUPER, died in Spanish Town, Jamaica, in 1800. [GM.70.905]

THE PEOPLE OF JAMAICA, 1655 TO 1855

BAYLY, DIANA SARAH, daughter of the late Nathaniel Bayly in Jamaica, married Reverend Samuel Holworthy, MA, of Croxhall, Derbyshire, in Cheshunt on 6 April 1811. [GM.81.392]

BAYLY, SOPHIA MARIA, daughter of the late N. Bayly of Bayly's Vale, Jamaica, married Thomas Raikes jr, in London on 24 May 1802. [GM.72.469]

BAYLY, Miss, daughter of the late Nathaniel Bayly in Jamaica, died in Bath on 29 April 1857. [GM.2/2.740]

BAYKY, ZACHARY, born 1721, Custos and Chief Magistrate of St Mary and St George, died 18 December 1769. [St Andrew's gravestone, Jamaica]

BAYNTUN, CHARLES, born 1814, eldest son of Edward Bayntun in Bronham, Wiltshire, died in Jamaica on 16 January 1833. [GM.103.479]

BAYNTUN, THOMAS, from Jamaica, married Miss Porter in Cheshunt on 4 November 1758. [GM.28.556]

BEACH, THOMAS, the Attorney General of Jamaica, died 1774. [GM.46.446]; died29 June 1774, husband of Helen, daughter of John Hynes, died 1771. [Chapleton gravestone, Claredon, Jamaica]

BEALL, Miss, of Lewisham, daughter of Edward Beall, late master shipwright in Jamaica, married Martin Morryson of Greenwich Hospital, in Lewisham, Kent, on 16 February 1788. [GM.58.178]

BEAMISH, THOMAS, a mariner from Aldgate, London, died aboard the Catherine in Jamaica, probate, 1700, PCC

BEAN, ANN, wife of Alexander Bean, born 1694, died 27 November 1726. [Kingston gravestone, Jamaica]

BEAN, JAMES, born 1778, nephew of John Bean in Kingston, died 24 December 1802. [Kingston gravestone, Jamaica]

THE PEOPLE OF JAMAICA, 1655 TO 1855

BEAN, JOHN, born 1806, died 6 August 1837. [Kingston gravestone, Jamaica]

BECKFORD, BALLARD, died in Jamaica on 23 May 1760. [GM.30.394]

BECKFORD, JULIERS, eldest son of Mr Beckford an estate owner in Jamaica, married Miss Ashey, daughter of Soloman Ashey MP, in Bridport on 17 January 1739. [GM.9.46]

BECKFORD, PETER, born 1643, Lieutenant Governor of Jamaica, 25 November 1697, [CSP.XI.66]; died 3 April 1710. [St Catherine's gravestone, Jamaica]

BECKFORD, PETER, from Jamaica, graduated from the University of Leyden in the Netherlands on 28 May 1725. [UL]

BECKFORD, PHILLIS, born 21 May 1708, daughter of Peter Beckford jr., died 8 May 1708. Also, son Peter, born 1734, died 16 August 1737. [St Catherine's gravestone, Jamaica]

BECKFORD, THOMAS, from Jamaica, married Mrs Burrel in Asted, Surrey, on 17 February 1745. [GM.15.108]

BECKFORD, WILLIAM, born 1690, son of George Beckford late of Ealing, Middlesex, died 11 December 1708. [St Catherine's gravestone, Jamaica]; a planter in Jamaica in 1758. [ActsPCCol.511]

BECKFORD, WILLIAM, from Jamaica, graduated from the University of Leyden in the Netherlands on 22 May 1817. [UL]

BECKFORD, Mr, and family from London, via Portsmouth aboard the New Duckinfield bound for Jamaica in 1774. [TNA.T47.9/11]

BEDWARD, GEORGE, jr., of Spring Garden Estate, Westmoreland, Jamaica, died aboard the Elizabeth on passage from Jamaica in 1787. [GM.57.837]

BEESTON, ELIZABETH, born 1675, daughter of Sir William Beeston, Governor of Jamaica, and his wife Ann, died 18 August 1693.

BEESTON, Sir WILLIAM, Governor of Jamaica, August 1692, [CSP.VIII.2412]; a proclamation against the Scots at Darien, 2 April 1699. [BM.Stowe.305, f238]

BEGBIE, JAMES, a shipbuilder in Charleston, S.C., a Loyalist in 1776, settled in Kingston, Jamaica, by 1784. [TNA.AO12.51.184, etc]

BEGG, JOHN, from Jamaica, graduated MD from Edinburgh University in 1793. [EMG.24]

BELFIELD, JOHN, a merchant in London, bound for Jamaica in 1664. [IRO.Deeds.I.20]; a merchant in Port Royal, dead by 1671. [IRO.Deeds.iii.229]

BELFOUR, Reverend HUGO JOHN, born 1802 in Jamaica, died there in September 1827. [GM.97.570]

BELL, HENRIETTE FRANCOISE, born 1811, died 25 October 1837. [Spring Path, Kingston, gravestone, Jamaica]

BELL, JOHN, Chief Justice in Portland, Jamaica, died in Kingston, Jamaica, on 19 July 1774. [GM.44.446]

BELL, RICHARD, a gentleman from London, died in Jamaica, 1657. [PCC]

BELL, General, born 1749, of Trelawney, Jamaica, died in London on 30 October 1816. [GM.86.471]

BENDFIELD, JOHN, gentleman in Jamaica, 1683, guardian of the children of Jacob Stokes, deceased. [IRO.Deeds.xvii.70]

BENNET, PAUL, a craftsman in Port Royal, 1673. [IRO.Deeds.xi.104]

BENNET, SAMUEL, in Jamaica, died 22 January 1755. [GM.25.43]

THE PEOPLE OF JAMAICA, 1655 TO 1855

BENTLEY, WILLIAM, born 1759, a gentleman from Surrey, bound via London aboard the Royal Charlotte for Jamaica in 1774. [TNA.T47.9/11]

BERMINGHAM, GERALD, of Athenry, Ireland, born 1694, died 11 December 1742. [St Catherine's gravestone, Jamaica]

BERNAL, JACOB ISRAEL, in Kingston, Jamaica, an indenture, 1782, [Car.3.158]; an indenture, 1798. [Car.3.25]

BERNAL, Mrs, widow of J. I. Bernal in Jamaica, died in London on 7 January 1832. [GM.102.92]

BERNARD, CHARLES, died in Jamaica in 1790. [GM.60.1148]

BERNARD, CHARLES EDWARD, MD, born in Jamaica, died in Bristol on 18 November 1842. [GM.ns19.93]; graduated MD from Edinburgh University in 1800. [EMG.31]

BERNARD, DANIEL P., from Jamaica, died 24 December 1816. [GM.87.374]

BERNARD, DAVID, husband of Judith, died 1804. [Montego Bay gravestone, Jamaica]

BERNARD, Mrs MARGARET, died 1781. [Montego Bay gravestone, Jamaica]

BERNARD, RACHEL, daughter of the late D. Bernard in Jamaica, died in Cheltenham on 2 March 1832. [GM.102.284]

BERNARD, SABINA, daughter of the late David Bernard, of Jamaica, married N. Atherton, a solicitor in London, on 20 April 1824. [GM.94.368]

BERNARD, SAMUEL, Governor of Jamaica, 30 June 1693, [CSP.IX.430]; in St Iago de la Vega, St Katherine's, Jamaica, probate, 1696, PCC; born 1636, Chief Justice, died 29 March 1695. [St Catherine's gravestone, Jamaica]

THE PEOPLE OF JAMAICA, 1655 TO 1855

BERNARD, THOMAS, father of John Bernard who died on 24 July 1720, and of Samuel Bernard, born 1718, died 17 November 1720. Also, Mary, born 1699, wife of Thomas Bernard, who died 13 August 1724. [St Catherine's gravestone, Jamaica]

BERNARD, THOMAS JAMES, a judge in St Anne's, Jamaica, died there on 3 March 1850. [GM.ns33.558]

BERRY, DOROTHY, wife of Curtis Philip Berry, died in Jamaica on 5 June 1835. [GM.ns4.335]

BERTHONNEAU, JOHN, died in Jamaica in 1791. [GM.61.186]

BERTRAND, JEAN-BAPTISTE, from Port Royal, Jamaica, to London, a journal, 1766. [Wiltshire Record Office]

BESLEY, JOSEPH, born 1751, a merchant from Barnstaple, bound for Jamaica in 1774. [TNA.T47.9/11]

BESLEY, OLIVER, born 1758, a merchant from Barnstaple, bound via Bristol for Jamaica in 1774. [TNA.T47.9/11]

BEST, ARTHUR, born 1800 in Hertford, died at Anotto Bay, Jamaica, in 1821. [GM.91.648]

BEST, GEORGE GRANVILLE, of HMS Imaum, born 1826, second son of the late Archdeacon Best in Fredericton, New Brunswick, died in Jamaica on 17 February 1849. [GM.ns31.558]

BETHUNE, GEORGE, an American Loyalist, probably from South Carolina, who was granted land in St Elizabeth parish in 1782. [TNA]

BETTS, JOHN, a gentleman from London, died in Jamaica, probate, 1697, PCC

BEWES, ..., third son of Thomas Bewes, MP for Plymouth, died in Jamaica on 30 June 1835. [GM.ns4.446]

THE PEOPLE OF JAMAICA, 1655 TO 1855

BEWLEY, Reverend T. H., General Superintendent of the Weslayan Mission Schools in Jamaica, died in Stewart's Town, Jamaica, on 14 July 1838. [GM.ns10.671]

BINHAM, GEORGE JAMES, from Jamaica, graduated MD from Edinburgh University in 1792. [EMG.23]

BINHAM, H., son of Dr Binham in Hanover, Jamaica, died on Iron Shore Wharf, Jamaica, on 22 June 1798. [GM.68.811]

BINNS, EDWARD, MD, died in Jamaica on 10 February 1851. [GM.ns35.574]

BIRBECK, WILLIAM, born 1758, a merchant's clerk from Cumberland, bound via Whitehaven aboard the Prince George for Jamaica in 1774. [TNA.T47.9/11]

BIRCH, BERNARD, born 1760 in Liverpool, died 1782. [Montego Bay gravestone, Jamaica]

BIRCH, RICHARD, late of Kingston, died in Falmouth, Jamaica, in November 1801. [GM.72.181]

BISHOP, THOMAS, from the Isle of Wight, died in Jamaica, admin., 1656, PCC

BIXTITH, GILBERT, from Liverpool, died in Jamaica, admin. 1656, PCC

BLACKMORE, FRANCIS, born 1658, son of Sir John Blackmore of Quantrix House, Somerset, died 24 October 1697. [St Catherine's gravestone, Jamaica]

BLACKMORE, GEORGE, born 1739, a merchant from Barnstaple, bound via Bristol for Jamaica in 1774. [TNA.T47.9/11]

BLAGROVE, ANN, born 1753, widow of John Blagrove, late in Jamaica, in London on 18 January 1834. [GM.104.228]

THE PEOPLE OF JAMAICA, 1655 TO 1855

BLAGROVE, CHARLES CAMPBELL, son of J. Blagrove of Cardiff Hall, Jamaica, died in Rotterdam in the Netherlands on 26 October 1815. [GM.82.671]

BLAGROVE, PETER, son of John Blagrove of Jamaica, died on Orange Valley Estate, St Anne's, Jamaica, in 1812. [GM.82.192]

BLAIR, ELIZA, born 1733, wife of Joseph Phipps a merchant in Kingston, Jamaica, died 30 June 1764. [St Andrew's gravestone, Jamaica]

BLAIR, Colonel JOHN, husband of Nideme, born 1678, died 5 March 1707. [St Catherine's gravestone, Jamaica]

BLAIR, JOHN, born 1668, died 27 June 1728, husband of Elizabeth, born 1694, died 7 July 1721, parents of John, Thomas, Christian and Mary. [St Catherine's gravestone, Jamaica]

BLAIR, JOHN, born 1716, son of Colonel John Blair, died 22 December 1742. [St Catherine's gravestone, Jamaica]

BLAIR, JOHN, a planter of 214 acres in St Andrew's parish in 1754. [TNA.CO137/28/171-196]

BLAIR, JOHN, born 1734, died 3 July 1764. [St Andrew's gravestone, Jamaica]

BLAIR, JOHN, formerly of Worthy Park, Jamaica, died in London on 15 December 1846. [GM.ns27.213]

BLAKE, JAMES, born 4 March 1753, died 1801. [Falmouth gravestone, Jamaica]

BLAKE, WILLIAM, born 1741, Speaker of the House of Assembly, died 24 January 1797. [St Catherine's gravestone, Jamaica]

BLICHENDON, ARTHUR, a planter in Jamaica, died 1780. [GM.50.155]

BINDLOSS, THOMAS, from Jamaica, graduated from the University of Leyden in The Netherlands on 23 August 1742. [UL]

THE PEOPLE OF JAMAICA, 1655 TO 1855

BLINSHALL, Mrs, widow of Thomas Blinshall in Clarendon, Jamaica, died in Hastings on 11 January 1802. [GM.72.93]

BLYTH, SARAH, born 1744, from London, bound via London aboard the Susanna for Jamaica in 1774. [TNA.T47.9/11]

BOELLE, DORA, died 6 August 1723. [St Michael's gravestone, Jamaica]

BOGLE, ALLAN JAMES, of Bogle and Company in Jamaica, was drowned in 1814. [GM.84.508]

BOLT, SARAH WALTERS, a free quadroon woman, and Edward Strudwick and Theodosia Strudwick, the reputed children of Henry Strudwick deceased, by the said Sarah Walters Bolt, an Act passed in Jamaica, giving them the same rights and privileges as English subjects. [JCTP:3.6.1777]

BONNER, JOHN, near Jamaica, probate, 1656, PCC

BONSALL, SAMUEL, born in England, settled in Charleston, South Carolina, as a blacksmith in 1766, a Loyalist, settled in Jamaica by 1784. [TNA.AO12.92.1a, etc]

BONTEIN, ARCHIBALD, observations on Kingston Harbour, Jamaica. [JCTP:21.5.1754]

BONTEIN, Mrs, wife of Thomas Bontein in Jamaica, died 10 June 1806. [GM.76.678]

BOOTH, ROBERT, the Assistant Commissary General, son of the late Reverend R. Booth in Rodmill, Jamaica, died in Jamaica on 1 November 1867. [GM.ns3/5.112]

BOOTH, THOMAS, in Jamaica, 8 November 1689. [TNA.Prob.4.5522]

BOSWELL, DAVID, died at Montego Bay, Jamaica, on 18 January 1790. [GM.60.372]

THE PEOPLE OF JAMAICA, 1655 TO 1855

BOUCHER, RICHARD, born 1754, died 12 December 1832 in Jamaica. [GM.103.190]

BOURDEN, JOHN, born in Coleraine, Ireland, in 1633, HM Councillor of Jamaica, died 18 August 1697. [St Catherine's gravestone, Jamaica]

BOURKE, JOHN, born 1776, late in Kingston, Jamaica, died in Knightsbridge, London, on 20 October 1814. [GM.84.503]

BOURKE, NICHOLAS, died in Jamaica in 1772. [GM.42.151]

BOUTCHER, ANTHONY, a gentleman in Port Royal, Jamaica, probate, 1682, will, 1688, PCC

BOWEN, JOSEPH, son of Joseph Bowen, died in Jamaica, on 4 September 1833. [GM.104.1181]

BOWEN, RICHARD LAWRENCE, died at Montego Bay, Jamaica, on 23 May 1829. [GM.99.94]

BOWERMAN, JOHANNA, born 1703, died 1729. [St Catherine's gravestone, Jamaica]

BOWLES, SIMON, from Wapping, London, died in Jamaica, probate, 1697, PCC

BOWROW, LEONARD, a mariner from County Durham, probate, 1699, PCC

BOWTEIN, THOMAS, from Jamaica, married Miss Cudden, daughter of Thomas Cudden, Master of Chancery, on 12 September 1777. [GM.47.459]

BOYD, MARY, from Jamaica, married Robert Kalley, a merchant in Glasgow, on 3 August 1795. [GM.65.702]

BRACE, JAMES, a planter, died in Clarendon, Jamaica, on 2 June 1795. [GM.65.791]

THE PEOPLE OF JAMAICA, 1655 TO 1855

BRADLEY, NATHANIEL, a yeoman from Scrooby, Nottinghamshire, died in Jamaica, probate, 1677, PCC

BRADLEY, THOMAS, from Bristol, died in Jamaica, probate, 1695, PCC

BRAGGE, WILLIAM, a merchant in London, bound for Jamaica in 1672. [IRO.Deeds.V.103]

BRAMFIELD, ANDREW, born 1741, formerly Lieutenant Colonel of Militia in Jamaica, died in Hoxton on 11 March 1807. [GM.77.383]

BRANDON, ABIGAIL, widow administratix of Isaac Pereira Brandon, a petitioner in Jamaica in 1752. [ActsPCCol.1745-1766.151]

BRAUMGAN, DENNIS, a merchant, died 9 December 1821. [Kingston gravestone, Jamaica]

BRAY, THOMAS, fought at the Battle of Sedgemoor in Somerset, on 6 July 1685 against the forces of King James II, captured and transported from Portland Road aboard the Jamaican Merchant of London, master Charles Gardiner, bound for Jamaica in 1685.

BRAYLEY, THOMAS, from Stepney, London, died in Jamaica, admin., PCC

BREAREY, Captain WALTER, son of the Mayor of York, died 29 November 1681. [St Catherine's gravestone, Jamaica]

BRERETON, ROBERT, died in Jamaica in 1790. [GM.60.1214]

BREWER, JOHN, born 1751, a merchant, bound via Bristol, aboard the Ann for Jamaica in 1775. [TNA.T47.9/11]

BREWSTER, THOMAS, born 1668, died 1701, his son Samuel Brewster, born 1692, died 1721. [St Catherine's gravestone, Jamaica]]

THE PEOPLE OF JAMAICA, 1655 TO 1855

BRIDGE, MARY, born 1716, died in Jamaica on 26 May 1827. [GM.97.477]

BRIDGES, DANIEL, born 1749, a merchant from Hull, via Hull aboard the Jamaica Packet bound for Jamaica in 1774. [TNA.T47.9/11]

BRIDGES, SAMUEL, a merchant from Southwark, London, died in Jamaica, probate, 1696, PCC

BRIDGEWOOD, ROBERT, a planter in the parish of St Elizabeth, Jamaica, probate 1680, PCC

BRILLOUET, JEANNE, a widow, born 1772, died 3 November 1832. [Spring Path gravestone, Kingston, Jamaica]

BRISCOE, ROBERT, in Jamaica, 1707. [ActsPCCol.1707.179]

BRISSET, Miss, daughter of J. Brisset in Jamaica, died in London on 25 December 1789. [GM.59.1214]

BROADBELT, FRANCIS RIGBY, born 9 October 1746, a physician, died 9 December 1795, father of Francis Rigby Broadbelt.   [St Catherine's gravestone, Jamaica]

BROADBELT, FRANCIS RIGBY, from Jamaica, graduated MD from Edinburgh University in 1794. [EMG.25]; married Miss Wilward, daughter of John Gardner Milward, in Spanish Town, Jamaica, on 25 July 1803. [GM.74.277]

BROADBETT, Miss, from Jamaica, married Captain Raymond of the 21st Light Dragoons, in Chadleigh, Devon, on 25 April 1798. [GM.68.441]

BROADGATES, ..., a sugar planter at Edward's Fort, St George's, Jamaica, attacked by Maroon rebels in 1734. [ActsPCCol.1735.440]

BROADSTREET, SAMUEL, died in Jamaica, admin., 1656, PCC

THE PEOPLE OF JAMAICA, 1655 TO 1855

BROCK, SUSAN MARGARET, daughter of W. W. Brock MD in Jamaica, married James Burnett former HM Consul in Brazil, in Torquay on 9 August 1860. [GM.ns2/9/318]

BROCK, W. W., born 1780, late in Jamaica, died in Clifden, Gloucestershire, on 10 November 1851. [GM.ns37.106]

BRODIE, OSWALD, of Flamstead Estate, died in St Ann's, Jamaica, on 9 August 1818. [GM.88.469]

BROMFIELD, Mrs ANN, wife of Jacob Bromfield in Kingston, died 28 June 1837; also, their daughter Ann, born December 1818, died 26 September 1819. [Spring Path, Kingston, gravestone, Jamaica]

BROOK, ANN, born 1717, from Westminster, via London aboard the Princess Carolina bound for Jamaica in 1774. [TNA.T47.9/11]

BROOKS, CAROLINE BROUGHTON, daughter of Dr Burt in Harwich, wife of Reverend George B. Brooks in Blenheim, Jamaica, died 14 December 1857. [GM.ns2/4.337]

BROOKS, CHARLES, a Representative at the Jamaican Assembly, died 1777. [GM.47.285]

BROOKS, GEORGE, MD, born 1810, died in Spanish Town, Jamaica, on 28 May 1854. [GM.ns2.201]

BROOKS, JOHN, the reputed son of George Brooks, in Jamaica, recommended to be given the same rights and privileges as an English subject. [JCTP; 19.6.1777]

BROOKSON, JAMES, born 1756, a gentleman from Surrey, via London aboard the Lady Tuliana bound for Jamaica in 1774. [TNA.T47.9/11]

BROOKSTEAD, ROBERT, died in Jamaica, admin., 1659, PCC

BROUGHTON, CAROLINE, born 1834, wife of Reverend George B. Brookes, died 14 December 1857. [St Andrew's gravestone, Jamaica]

THE PEOPLE OF JAMAICA, 1655 TO 1855

BROUGHTON, WILLIAM, died in Jamaica, admin., 1656, PCC

BROWNE, Mrs ANNE, born 1775, only daughter of John White in Jamaica, wife of Lieutenant Colonel John Browne, died in Bath on 23 April 1851. [GM.April 1851]

BROWN, ELEANOR, born 1768, died 18 March 1808. [Spring Path gravestone, Kingston, Jamaica]

BROWN, HENRY, a barrister, died in Jamaica in 1790. [GM.60.476]

BROWN, HENRY, sr., died in Jamaica in 1790. [GM.60.766]

BROWN, JAMES, and his wife Ann Mellor, parents of Mary died 1791, Anne died 1794, Abner died 1794, and William died 1800, all infants. [Kingston gravestone, Jamaica]

BROWN, JOHN, a mariner from Shadwell, Middlesex, died aboard the Agreement in Jamaica, probate, 1696, PCC

BROWN, JOHN ROBERT, from Jamaica, married Elizabeth, daughter of John Holder of Cubberly House, Hereford, in Bath on 19 December 1848. [GM.ns31.310]

BROWN, LETITIA, born 1769, wife of John Brown of Sportsmanhall, Trelawney, Jamaica, died in Bristol on 30 May 1817. [GM.87.571]

BROWN, MARY ANNE FULLER, daughter of John Fuller Brown of Mulberry Garden, married Joseph Johnstone from Bengal, in Spanish Town, Jamaica, in 1797. [GM.97.710]

BROWN, MARY ANN, wife of Daniel Brown, died 1819. [Falmouth gravestone, Jamaica]

BROWN, MARY ANNE FULLER, daughter of John Fuller Brown of Mulberry Gardens, Spanish Town, Jamaica, married Joseph Johnstone in Bengal in 1797. [GM.67.710]

BROWNE, MARY ISABELLA, widow of James Browne, the Customs Controller of Savanna la Mar, Jamaica, married Lieutenant

THE PEOPLE OF JAMAICA, 1655 TO 1855

Frederick Jelly of the Royal Navy, in Hatfield Pen, Savanna la Mar, Jamaica, on 11 October 1820. [GM.91.83]

BROWNE, OTWAY CUFFE, third son of the Dean of Fens, died in Jamaica in 1836, [GM.ns6.446]

BROWN, T. JAMES, born 1792, an Assemblyman in Jamaica, died on passage to England, on 20 April 1823. [GM.93.478]

BROWN, WILLIAM, born 1750, a gentleman from London, from London aboard the Lady's Adventure bound for Jamaica in 1776. [TNA.T47.9/11]

BROWN, WILLIAM PATRICK, Chief Magistrate, Major General of Militia, and Colonel of the St Catherine's Regiment, died in Brown's Hall, Jamaica, in 1789. [GM.59.372]

BROWN, WILLIAM, born 1764, Rear Admiral of the Red and Commander in Chief in Jamaica, died 20 September 1814. [Kingston gravestone, Jamaica]

BRUEKNALL, WILLIAM, late in Jamaica, died 22 September 1746. [GM.16.558]

BRYAN, SAMUEL, a mariner aboard HMS Rupert died in Jamaica, probate, 1695, PCC

BRYAN, Reverend, of Machioneal, died in Jamaica, in 1790. [GM.60.1214]

BRYNE, ANDREW, died in Jamaica in 1781. [GM.61.871]

BUCKNAM, JOHN THOMAS, a mariner from Ipswich, died in Jamaica, probate, 1656, PCC

BULKLEY, MORRIS PEAT, born 1791, died 24 May 1808. [Spring Path, Kingston, gravestone, Jamaica]

BULL, ELEANOR, born 1788, daughter of John and Sarah Bull, died 9 July 1792. [Kingston gravestone, Jamaica]

THE PEOPLE OF JAMAICA, 1655 TO 1855

BULL, JOHN, died at Montego Bay, Jamaica, on 31 October 1801. [GM.72.18]

BULLOCK, DOROTHY, only daughter of E. Bullock in Jamaica, married Reverend John Bowen of St Vincent, only son of Rear Admiral J. Bowen of Ilfracombe, Devon, in St George's, Bloomsbury, London, on 27 April 1830. [GM.100.400]

BULLOCK, EDMUND, from Jamaica married Dorothy Harrison, daughter of Thomas Harrison, late Attorney General of Jamaica, in Bath in 1796. [GM.66.789]

BULLOCK, MARY PENNINGTON, daughter of Edmund Bullock in Jamaica, married Reverend Frederick Bell of Clifton, son of Dr Thomas Bell in Dublin, at Clifton on 16 March 1843. [GM.ns19.528]

BULLOCK, RICHARD, born 1809, son of Edmund Bullock late in Jamaica, died in Windsor on 3 April 1847. [GM.96.474]

BUNNETT, EDWARD CHARLES, born 1819, son of Henry James Bunnett MD, died in Spanish Town, Jamaica, on 10 May 1854. [GM.ns42.201]

BUNTING, Reverend GEORGE ANTHONY, born 1839, son of Reverend Anthony Bunting, Port Antonio, Jamaica, died in Leicester on 31 My 1855. [GM.ns44.104]

BUNTING, Mrs JANE ELIZABETH, widow of Reverend Anthony Bunting of Port Antonio, Jamaica, died in Newport Pagnell on 9 January 1857. [GM.ns2/2.254]

BURGE, BENJAMIN MILWARD, born 1796, a barrister, died in Spanish Town on 16 June 1819. [St Catherine's gravestone, Jamaica] [GM.89.185]

BURGE, WILLIAM, HM Counsel in Jamaica, married Margaret, daughter of Reverend Archibald Alison in Edinburgh on 11 August 1841. [GM.ns16.424]

THE PEOPLE OF JAMAICA, 1655 TO 1855

BURGER, RICHARD, born 1790, died 12 January 1842. [Kingston gravestone, Jamaica]

BURKE, EDWARD, born 1759, died 8 April 1807. . [Spring Path, Kingston, gravestone]

BURKE, JOHN, from Kingston, Jamaica, died in Brighton, on 13 December 1824. [GM.95.190]

BURNABY, Sir WILLIAM, in Jamaica, a letter, 1765. [HMC.24]

BURNETT, ... , a planter of 502 acres in St Andrew's parish in 1754. [TNA.CO137/28/171-196]

BURNSIDE, THOMAS, a planter of 480 acres in St Andrew's parish in 1754. [TNA.CO137/28/171-196]

BURROWS, CHARLES, died in Jamaica in 1767. [GM.37.524]

BURTENSHAW, ..., son of Henry Burtenshaw in Lewes, died in Jamaica on 4 September 1794. [GM.64.1150]

BURTON, HARRIET EMMA, daughter of Reverend William Burton in Trelawney, Jamaica, married Charles A. Cunningham MD from London, in Upton, Buckinghamshire, on 15 September 1852. [GM.ns38.630]

BURTON, Reverend WILLIAM, from Horsfield, Norwich, died at Montego Bay on 12 December 1808. [GM.79.278]

BURTON, Reverend W. G. P., son of Reverend W. Brton in St Thomas in the Vale, died in Spanish Town, Jamaica, on 29 July 1847. [GM.ns28.549]

BUSHBY, JOSEPH, Deputy Commissary General of St Domingo, died in Jamaica in April 1799. [GM.69.716]

BUSHMAN, HENRY, born 1804, son of James Bushman, died 21 June 1810. [St Andrew's gravestone, Jamaica]

THE PEOPLE OF JAMAICA, 1655 TO 1855

BUSSELL, ANNE, wife of W. I. Bussell, died in Jamaica on 8 November 1852. [GM.ns39.216]

BUTFIELD, JOHN, fought at the Battle of Sedgemoor in Somerset, on 6 July 1685 against the forces of King James II, captured and transported from Portland Road aboard the Jamaican Merchant of London, master Charles Gardiner, bound for Jamaica in 1685.

BUTTERY, JAMES, died in Jamaica, admin., 1658, PCC

BYAM, Sir ASHTON, the Attorney General of Jamaica, died on 25 December 1790. [GM.61.184]

BYNDLOS, Colonel ROBERT, born 1637, died 16 July 1687. [St Catherine's gravestone, Jamaica]

CALDWELL, WILLIAM, Assemblyman for St Dorothy's and an Alderman of Kingston, died in Kingston, Jamaica, on 29 January 1810. [GM.88.376]

CALLAGHAN, CATHERINE, daughter of H. Callaghan of Pusey Hall, Vere, Jamaica, married Reginald Henry Elliot, son of James Elliot of Dymchurch, Essex, in Vere on 16 September 1863. [GM.ns2/15.635]

CAMERON, ALEXANDER, an American Loyalist, probably from South Carolina, who was granted land in St Elizabeth parish in 1782. [TNA]

CAMERON, ALLAN, died in Kingston, Jamaica, on 27 May 1796. [GM.66.615]

CAMERON, ANGUS, an American Loyalist, probably from South Carolina, who was granted land in St Elizabeth parish in 1782. [TNA]

CAMERON, DONALD, an American Loyalist, probably from South Carolina, who was granted land in St Elizabeth parish in 1782. [TNA]

THE PEOPLE OF JAMAICA, 1655 TO 1855

CAMERON, Dr, died in Kingston, Jamaica, on 23 August 1800. [GM.70.1214]

CAMPBELL, ANGUS, an American Loyalist, probably from South Carolina, who was granted land in St Elizabeth parish in 1782. [TNA]

CAMPBELL, Major General ARCHIBALD, Governor and Commander in Chief of Jamaica, a memorandum on the military state of Jamaica, 1782. [BM.King's.214]

CAMPBELL, CATHERINE, daughter of Reverend John Campbell in St Andrew's, Jamaica, widow of Dr W. B. Seaman in Vere, Jamaica, died in Teignmouth on 10 April 1864. [GM.ns2/16.810]

CAMPBELL, COLIN, an American Loyalist, probably from South Carolina, who was granted land in St Elizabeth parish in 1782. [TNA]

CAMPBELL, DANIEL, a planter of 98 acres in St Andrew's parish in 1754. [TNA.CO137/28/171-196]

CAMPBELL, DONALD, an American Loyalist, probably from South Carolina, who was granted land in St Elizabeth parish in 1782. [TNA]

CAMPBELL, PETER, an American Loyalist, probably from South Carolina, who was granted land in St Elizabeth parish in 1782. [TNA]

CAMPBELL, THOMAS, born 1748, a stationer from Penrith, bound via Whitehaven aboard the Prince George for Jamaica in 1774. [TNA.T47.9/11]

CAPPELL, Mrs, widow of William Cappell in Jamaica, died in Yarmouth in 1814. [GM.84.99]

CARDOZO, ABRAHAM RODRIQUEZ, born 1703, died 1791 in Jamaica, [GM.61.682]

THE PEOPLE OF JAMAICA, 1655 TO 1855

CARDROSSO, MOSES JUSSURAN, probate December 1725

CAREY, WILLIAM, born 1780, of the Water Wheel in Westmoreland, Jamaica, died in Winchester on 24 November 1842. [GM.ns19.106]

CARLISLE, Lord CHARLES, Governor of Jamaica, 1680. [CSP.V.1570]

CARMICART, ELIZABETH, born 1759, from London, bound via London aboard the Royal Charlotte for Jamaica in 1774. [TNA.T47.9/11]

CARPENTER, PHILIP, a merchant in Jamaica, died in 1769. [GM.39.270]

CARR, Mrs MARY, born 1770, wife of Dawkins Carr the commander of the Jupiter, died 4 June 1798. [Kingston gravestone, Jamaica]

CARR, THOMAS, a merchant, son of John Carr a watch-manufacturer in Coventry, died in Jamaica on 12 June 1807. [GM.77.780]

CARRELL, PATRICK, from Galway, Ireland, a mariner aboard the Gilbert and Ann, died in Jamaica, probate, 1697, PCC

CARRUTHERS, GEORGE, son of James Carruthers of Dunwoodie Green, died on Dundee Estate, Trelawney, on 15 July 1796. [GM.66.880]

CARTER, AMBROSE, from Jamaica, graduated MD from Edinburgh University in 1794. [EMG.25]

CARTER, ELLEN, daughter of William Carter in Troy, Jamaica, married Lieutenant Colonel G. W. G. Green of the 2nd East Bengal Fusiliers, in London on 16 June 1859. [GM.ns2/9.82]

CARTWRIGHT, WILLIAM, born 1751, a cordwainer from London, , via London aboard the Nancy bound for Jamaica in 1774. [TNA.T47.9/11]

CARY, JAMES, settled on the Wateree River, Craven County, South Carolina, around 1762, a Loyalist soldier, moved to Jamaica in January 1783. [TNA.AO12.49.60, etc]

CARY, LUCIUS, from Jamaica, died in Clifton on 26 August 1826. [GM.96.284]

CARY, Colonel THEODORE, of Cockington House, Devon, born 1620, brother of Sir Henry Cary commander of the fort at Port Royal, died 26 June 1683.   [St Catherine's gravestone, Jamaica]

CASTILLO, JAMES, Agent in Jamaica for the Asiento, 16... [JHR.viii.11]

CEAN, JAMES, an Assemblyman, died in Kingston, Jamaica, in 1781. [GM.51.489]

CELESTIN, JEAN LOUIS, born 1807, died 16 January 1830. [Spring Path gravestone, Kingston, Jamaica]

CERF, AMELIA, from Jamaica, daughter of Henry Cerf of Worton Hall, married M. Deby, a barrister from Brussels, in Bath on 9 February 1825. [GM.95.177]

CERF, HENRY, born 1757, late of Isleworth and of Jamaica, died in Brussels on 18 November 1840. [GM.ns15.110]

CHAFFERS, JAMES, born 1740, a gentleman and a merchant from Wales, bound for Jamaica via Liverpool aboard the St Peter in 1773. [TNA.T47.9/11]

CHALMERS, GILBERT, in Charleston, South Carolina, a Loyalist, moved to Kingston, Jamaica, by 1783. [TNA.AO12.92.1A, etc]

CHAMBERS, JOHN, brother of Edward Chambers in Devon, died in Jamaica in 1770. [GM.40.344]

THE PEOPLE OF JAMAICA, 1655 TO 1855

CHAMBERS, JOHN, born 1752, a gentleman from London, bound via London aboard the Henry for Jamaica in 1774. [TNA.T47.9/11]

CHAMBERS, JOHN THARP, son of Edward Chambers, died 1795. [Falmouth gravestone, Jamaica]

CHAMBERS, Miss, daughter of Edward Chambers of Bachelor's Hall, Jamaica, married James Weeks jr., in Bristol on 4 July 1782. [GM.62.672]

CHAMBERLAIN, ROBERT, born 1802, son of Robert Chamberlain of Millet Estate, Jamaica, died in London on 28 October 1821. [GM.91.477]

CHAMBERLAIN, SAMUEL, born 1714, from St Ann's, Jamaica, died in London on 17 February 1794. [GM.64.281]

CHANDLER, ...,daughter of Major Chandler of the Royal Artillery, was born in Jamaica on 27 September 1863. [GM.ns2/15.769]

CHAPLYN, ISAAC, from Wareham, Dorset, died in Jamaica, admin., 1656, PCC

CHAPMAN, Mrs SARAH, born 1729, died 29 June 1803. [Kingston gravestone, Jamaica]

CHAPMAN, WILLIAM BLOOM, born 1776, son of Deputy Chapman in London, died in Jamaica in 1794. [GM.64.1155]

CHARLTON, CHARLES HENRY, son of Captain John Charlton of the Royal Artillery, died in Jamaica on 12 November 1841. [GM.ns17.231]

CHARNLEY, WILLIAM, son of .... Charnley in Blackburn, the Coroner of Lancashire, died in Jamaica in 1795. [GM.65.880]

CHARNOCK, JOHN, MD, died 30 September 1730, husband of Frances – daughter of Captain John Rose in London, parents of

Elizabeth 1711-1720, and Mary 1716-1720. [St John's gravestone, Jamaica]

CHARNOCKE, MARY, daughter of Laurence and Sarah Charnocke, wife of George Modd, died 10 February 1709. [St John's gravestone, Jamaica]

CHARRIER, MARIE CELESTINE, born 1783, died 27 August 1823. [Spring Path gravestone, Kingston, Jamaica]

CHERRY, FREDERICK, born 1758, died 22 April 1798. [Kingston gravestone, Jamaica]

CHERTON, CAROLINE MARIA, daughter of Reverend John Cherton in, Worcestershire, wife of Reverend Charles Cooper, died in Jamaica on 9 July1843. [GM.ns20.446]

CHILDERMAS, JOHN, born 1666, died 1699. [St Catherine's gravestone, Jamaica]

CHISHAM, THOMAS, born 1759, a clerk from London, via London aboard the Lady Tuliana bound for Jamaica in 1774. [TNA.T47.9/11]

CHISHOLM, JOHN, born in Ross-shire, Scotland, to America in 1757 as a soldier of the 77th Regiment, settled in Camden, South Carolina, as a merchant, a Loyalist soldier, moved to Kingston, Jamaica, by 1783. [TNA.AOO12.49.417, etc]

CHISHOLM, Dr, born 1745, a physician, returning via London aboard the James Daukins for Jamaica in 1774. [TNA.T47.9/11]

CHOVET, ABRAHAM, MD, born 1704, settled in Jamaica, moved to Philadelphia in 1770, died there on 24 March 1790. [GM.61.279]

CHRISTIANSON, CHRISTIAN, a mariner from Shadwell, Middlesex, died aboard the Tiger, probate, 1694, PCC

CHRISTIE, Miss, niece of Fairley Christie the Assemblyman for Kingston, Jamaica, married Michael Parys in July 1800. [GM.70.1001]

CHUSEMAN, FRANCIS, a gentleman from London, died in Jamaica, probate, 1685, PCC

CLACKTON, JOSEPH, in Jamaica, died 9 September 1763. [GM.33.565]

CLARE, MICHAEL BENIGNUS, MD, Physician General of Jamaica, married Margaret Graham, daughter of Colonel C. D. Graham, in Twickenham Park, Jamaica, on 18 March 1817. [GM.87.465]

CLARK, Sir ALURED, Lieutenant Governor of Jamaica, letter in Jamaica, died at the Deanery, Wolverhampton in 1838. [GM.ns59.669][book, 1784-1790. NLW.Rhual7]

CLARK, DAVID, of Rouse and Clarke merchants, died in Jamaica on 3 June 1818. [GM.88.373]

CLARK, EDWARD, was appointed a Councillor of Jamaica in 1759. [JCTP; 11.8.1759]

CLARKE, EDWARD, of Trelawney, Jamaica, dead by 1777, estates then managed by William Atherton. [Lancashire Record Office, DDPr.32/1-4]

CLARKE, ELIZABETH ANNE, born 1804, daughter of Josias Clarke in Jamaica, died at Hotwells on 16 July 1825. [GM.95.189]

CLARKE, FRANCES, SHIRLEY CLARKE, ANN CLARKE, ROBERT PAWLETT CLARKE, THOMAS CLARKE, and WILLIAM CLARKE, the reputed children of Robert Clarke, a gentleman in the parish of St Catherine, Jamaica, and Charlotte Pawlett a free mulatto woman, to be entitled to the same rights and privileges of English subjects. [JCTP;10.7.1777] [St Lucea gravestone, Hanover, Jamaica]

CLARK, GEORGE, in Jamaica, 1707. [ActsPCCol.1707.179]

CLARK, J., in Jamaica, 1708. [ActsPCCol.1708.202]

CLARKE, JOHN, from Jamaica died 16 February 1813. [GM.84.410]

CLARKE, JOHN GARDINER, born 1827, of H.M.Customs, died 26 June 1850. [St Andrew's gravestone, Jamaica]

CLARKE, JOSEPH CHARLES, of Jamaica, died in Brighton on 12 November 1828. [GM.98.476]

CLARKE, RICHARD, a merchant from Fleet Street, London, died in Jamaica, probate, 1700, PCC

CLARK, RICHARD, born 1744, a cooper from London, bound via London aboard the Mars for Jamaica in 1774. [TNA.T47.9/11]

CLARKE, Sir SIMON, born in Jamaica in 1727, died 2 November 1777. [GM]

CLARKE, W., born 1756, a gentleman returning to Jamaica via London aboard the New Shoreham in 1774. [TNA.T47.9/11]

CLAYTON, ARTHUR, died in Jamaica, admin., 1659, PCC

CLAYTON, GEORGE, died 3 April 1816. [Kingston gravestone, Jamaica]

CLEATON, ROBERT JAMES, born 1753 from London, bound via London aboard the Fanny for Jamaica in 1774. [TNA.T47.9/11]

CLEMENT, ANNE, born 1732, daughter of John Clement of Petersfield, Southampton, wife of George Ramsay the Registrar in Chancery, died 14 August 1764. [St Catherine's gravestone, Jamaica]

CLEMENTS, Mrs CHARLOTTE, born 1807, died 18 July 1844. [Annotto Bay gravestone, Jamaica]

CLEMENTS, WILLIAM, a merchant in Port Royal, 1671. [IRO.III.207]

THE PEOPLE OF JAMAICA, 1655 TO 1855

CLIEFE, WILLIAM, born 1813, son of Thomas Cliefe, and nephew of J. Cliefe of Yorkhill Castle, Herefordshire, the Customs Collector at Morant, Jamaica, died there in 1841. [GM.ns15.670]

CLIFFORD, FRANCIS, from Barking, Essex, died in Jamaica, admin.,1658, PCC

CLUTSAM, GEORGE, born 1793, son of Captain G. Clutsam, was downed in Jamaica on 14 June 1813. [GM.83.194]

CLOWES, DAWSON, born 1721, midshipman aboard HMS Maidstone died 3 December 1737. [Kingston gravestone, Jamaica]

COALE, GEORGE, a merchant, late of Port Royal, Jamaica, died in London, probate, 1683, PCC

COATES, Reverend HENRY, born 1831, formerly of Worcester College, Oxford, died in Spanish Town, Jamaica, on 28 July 1853. [GM.ns41.214]

CODRINGTON, ANNE, daughter of John Codrington in Manchioneal, married James Tyrrell, in Portland, Jamaica, on 23 June 1792. [GM.62.1151]

COHEN, ANDREW, died in Jamaica in 1790. [GM.60.1214]

COLBECK, Colonel JOHN, of Colbeck in St Dorothy's, born 30 May 1630, came with the army in 1655, died 22 February 1682. [St Catherine's gravestone, Jamaica]

COLE, HERBERT, born 1756, a gentleman from Paddington, via London aboard the Princess Carolina bound for Jamaica in 1774. [TNA.T47.9/11]

COLE, MARY, born 1735, died 11 February 1799. [Windsor Estate gravestone, St Ann's, Jamaica]

COLE, THOMAS, a mariner from Stepney, London, died aboard the merchant ship Mary and Margaret in Jamaica, probate, 1699, PCC

THE PEOPLE OF JAMAICA, 1655 TO 1855

COLETTE, VICTOIRE ADELE, born 1801, died 12 September 1827. [Spring Path gravestone, Kingston, Jamaica]

COLLEY, HUGH, a merchant in Jamaica, 1669, deceased. [IRO.Deeds.iii.128-130]

COLLYER, ANTHONY, born 1637 in Gloucester, died 10 August 1677. [St Catherine's gravestone, Jamaica]

COLPEPPER, FRANCIS, born 1717 in Hollingbourn, Kent, died 1761. [St Catherine's gravestone, Jamaica]

COLQUHOUN, GEORGE, an American Loyalist, probably from South Carolina, who was granted land in St Elizabeth parish in 1782. [TNA]

COMBE, JAMES, , fought at the Battle of Sedgemoor in Somerset, on 6 July 1685 against the forces of King James II, captured and transported from Portland Road aboard the Jamaican Merchant of London, master Charles Gardiner, bound for Jamaica in 1685.

COMPERE, LEONARD, was granted the office of Receiver General by King Charles II on 3 April 1674, [APCCol.27]; a petition 26 February 1701, [APCCol.27]; Receiver General of Jamaica. [JCTP;11.4.1704]

CONCANEN, MATTHEW, former Attorney General of Jamaica, died 22 January1749. [GM.19.44]

COOK, HENRY, born 1757, a gentleman from London, bound via London aboard the Ashley for Jamaica in 1774. [TNA.T47.9/11]

COOK, MARK, born 1756, a merchant's clerk from Hull, bound via Hull aboard the Jamaica Packet for Jamaica in 1774. [TNA.T47.9/11]

COOLEY, MATTHEW, died in Jamaica, probate, 22 September 1692, PCC; [TNA.Prob.11.411.304]

THE PEOPLE OF JAMAICA, 1655 TO 1855

COOPER, Reverend CHARLES ALFRED, born in Newport, Shropshire, in 1819, minister in St Thomas in the East, died 19 June 1853. [Kingston gravestone, Jamaica]

COOPER, JANE, born 1663, died 1749. [St Catherine's gravestone, Jamaica]

COOPER, SAMUEL, born 1788, son of Robert Cooper in Woodbridge, Suffolk, died in Jamaica on 15 June 1814. [GM.84.292]

COORE, Mrs ISABELLA, born 1786, daughter of John Blagrove in Jamaica, died in London in 1831. [GM.101.187]

COPE, ESTHER, a widow of St John's parish, Jamaica, and St Faith parish, London, probate, 1692, PCC

COPE, JOHN, born 1725, a judge of the Supreme Court, died in Westmoreland, Jamaica, on 1 March 1792. [GM.62.479]

COPE, JOHN, an attorney and clerk of the peace in Westmoreland, Jamaica, died in Kingston, Jamaica, in 1793. [GM.63.1152]

COPE, JOSEPH, a cooper died aboard the Catherine in Jamaica, probate, 1697, PCC

COPE, Colonel, Governor of Placentia, died in Jamaica, in 1742. [GM.13.51]

CORD, THOMAS, a mariner aboard the frigate Laurel at Jamaica, probate, 1656, PCC

CORDOSA, MOSES JESURUM, in Port Royal, 1677. [IRO.Deeds.viii.87]

CORKER, Mrs DEBORAH, born 4 November 1707, daughter of Dr John Burnell, wife of T. Corker, died 29 October 1727. [St John's gravestone, Jamaica]

COSENS, Mrs GRACE, widow of Gied. H. Cosens in Jamaica, died in Exeter in December 1821. [GM.91.647]

COTTON, Reverend FRANCIS, formerly a schoolmaster in Jamaica, wished to return there as a clergyman, 1720. [Bodleian Library, Rawlinson.]

COULSON, SAMUEL, a merchant from London, died in Jamaica, probate, 1689, PCC

COX, HENRY, born 1776, Assemblyman for St Mary's, and Custos Rotulorum of St Anne's, Jamaica, died in Devonport on 20 December 1844. [GM.ns23.215]

COX, Mrs LETITIA, born 1678, died in Bybrook, Jamaica, on 26 June 1838. [GM.ns10.454]

COXON, JOHN, a buccaneer residing in High Street, Port Royal, 1680s. [IRO. Deeds.xvii.75]

COXSHOT, ABRAHAM, a cabinetmaker, an inventory, 1683. [Jamaica Archives, inventories, II]

CRAIG, ROBERT, an American Loyalist, probably from South Carolina, who was granted land in St Elizabeth parish in 1782. [TNA]

CRANDALL, WILLIAM, a merchant in London, died in Jamaica, probate, 1682, PCC, B376.P234]

CRANE, GILES, fought at the Battle of Sedgemoor in Somerset, on 6 July 1685 against the forces of King James II, captured and transported from Portland Road aboard the <u>Jamaican Merchant of London</u>, master Charles Gardiner, bound for Jamaica in 1685.

CRANE, WILLIAM, a merchant in Queen Street, Port Royal, before 1692. [IRO.Deeds vi.17/viii.246]

CRASKELL,ROBERT, died in Jamaica in 1799. [GM.60.1053]

CRASSWELL, JOSEPH, born 1729, died 1768. [St Catherine's gravestone, Jamaica]

CRAWFORD, LAURENCE, in Jamaica, married Patty Redman from London, in May 1750. [GM.20.284]

CRIEF, JOHN, a saddler from London, emigrating via Portsmouth aboard the Thetis bound for Jamaica in 1776. [TNA.T47.9/11]

CROASDAILE, EDWARD, from Jamaica, graduated MD from Edinburgh University in 1799. [EMG.30]

CROASDAILE, THOMAS, died 10 October 1752. [St Andrew's gravestone, Jamaica]

CROOKS, RICHARD, from Jamaica, graduated MD from Edinburgh University in 1793. [EMG.24]

CROSS, RICHARD, born 1736, a distiller from Paddington, via London aboard the Princess Carolina bound for Jamaica in 1774. [TNA.T47.9/11]

CROSSE, THOMAS, fought at the Battle of Sedgemoor in Somerset, on 6 July 1685 against the forces of King James II, captured and transported from Portland Road aboard the Jamaican Merchant of London, master Charles Gardiner, bound for Jamaica in 1685.

CROSSMAN, JAMES, died in Jamaica in 1791. [GM.61.186]

CROWDEN, SAMUEL, born 1752, a grocer from London, bound via London aboard the Royal Charlotte for Jamaica in 1774. [TNA.T47.9/11]

CROWTHER, Reverend G. D., died in Jamaica on 12 September 1848. [GM.ns30.663]

CRUGER, Mr, jr., born 1747, a farrier from London, bound via London aboard the James Daukins for Jamaica in 1774. [TNA.T47.9/11]

CRUGER, Mr, born 1744, a planter, returning via London aboard the James Daukins for Jamaica in 1774. [TNA.T47.9/11]

CUMINE, ALEXANDER, a minister in South Carolina from 1764 to 1777, also a schoolmaster in Beaufort, Port Royal, moved to Kingston, Jamaica, as a schoolmaster. [TNA.AO12.49.422, etc]

CUMMING, THOMAS, born 1760, a merchant, died 29 July 1815. [Kingston gravestone, Jamaica]

CUNNINGHAM, HENRY, born 1677, Governor of Jamaica, died 12 February 1735. [St Catherine's gravestone, Jamaica]

CUNNINGHAM, SAMUEL, born 1756, a gentleman returning to Jamaica via London aboard the William and Mary in 1774. [TNA.T47.9/11]

CUNSTANCE, Mrs ELIZABETH, born 1797, daughter of J. White in Paulsgrove, Hampshire, died in Spanish Town, Jamaica, on 28 May 1822. [GM.92.382]

CURRY, JAMES, an American Loyalist, probably from South Carolina, who was granted land in St Elizabeth parish in 1782. [TNA]

CURTIN, SAMUEL, from Jamaica, graduated MD from Edinburgh University in 1778. [EMG.14]

CURTIS, ROBERT, died in Jamaica, admin., 1655, PCC

CUTHBERT, THOMAS, an American Loyalist, probably from South Carolina, who was granted land in St Elizabeth parish in 1782. [TNA]

DA COSTA, DANIEL MENDES, a petitioner in Jamaica, 1752, [ActsPCCol.1745-1766.151]; in Jamaica, probate, 1755, PCC

DA COSTA, ISAAC MENDES, in Jamaica, probate, 1766, PCC

DA COSTA, ISAAC RODRIGUEZ, in Jamaica, probate, 1805, PCC

DA COSTA, REBECCA MENDES, in Jamaica, probate, 1804, PCC

DADLEY, JAMES, born 1808, from Bath, died at Barking Lodge, Jamaica, in 1839. [GM.ns13.110]

D'AGUILAR, BENJAMIN, in Jamaica, probate, 1813, PCC

D'AGUILAR, REBECCA, in Jamaica, probate, 1810, PCC

DALLAS, CHARLES ROBERT KING, from Jamaica, late of the 22nd Regiment, married Julia Maria Dallas, daughter of Robert Charles Dallas of St Adriesse, Normandy, France, also of Jamaica, in Paris on 3 July 1821. [GM.91.85]

DALLAS, ROBERT, a planter of 900 acres in St Andrew's parish in 1754. [TNA.CO137/28/171-196]

DALLAS, ROBERT, married Mrs John Hewitt a widow, in Jamaica on 20 April 1769. [GM.39.215]

DALLAS, SUSAN SEIL, born 1770, widow of Charles Stuart Dallas of Belle Cou, Jamaica, died at Stratton, Cornwall, on 20 August 1843. [GM.ns20.554]

DANCER, THOMAS, MD, a physician and a botanist, died in Kingston, Jamaica, on 1 August 1811. [GM.81.390]

DANCY, MATHEW, died in Jamaica, admin., 1656, PCC

DANIELL, J., in Jamaica, a letter, 1655. [Bodleian, Rawlinson.A27.47]

DANSEY, ARTHUR, died in Jamaica, admin., 1656, PCC

DANVERS, THOMAS, Vice Admiral of the Red, died 16 September 1746. [St Andrew's gravestone, Jamaica]

DARBY, JOHN, born 1744, died 5 April 1799. [Spring Path gravestone, Kingston, Jamaica]

DARE, JEFFREY BEARE, in Jamaica, letters, 1656. [Bodleian, Rawlinson ms A42.25; A43.111]

DASHWOOD, Mr, Postmaster, died in Jamaica in 1790. [GM.63.866]

DA SILVA, EZEKIA LOPEZ, probate, 7 December 1759.

DA SILVA, SHELLAMONT, husband of [1] Christian died 12 September 1827, and [2] Mary Anne died 27 March 1854. [St Andrew's gravestone, Jamaica]

DAUNCEY, Reverend FRANCIS, in St James, Jamaica, died at Montego Bay on 28 April 1795. [GM.65.614]

DA VEIGA, SAMUEL B., in Jamaica, probate, 1812, PCC

DAVENPORT, JOHN, a merchant in Jamaica in 1670. [IRO.Deeds.iii.108]

DAVIES, DECIMA ISABELLA CATHERINE, daughter of Thomas Davies, MD, in Newbattle, Jamaica, married Charles Inman, son of Charles Inman in Liverpool, at East Barnet on 15 September 1853. [GM.ns40.628]

DAVIS, EDWARD, born 1757, a gentleman from London, via London aboard the Great Marlow bound for Jamaica in 1774. [TNA.T47.9/11]

DAVIS, JAMES, in St Elizabeth's, Jamaica, probate, 1694.

DAVIS, MARIA, widow of Henry Davis a Customs Collector, died in Jamaica in August 1845. [GM.ns.24.665]

DAWKINS, Mrs ELIZABETH, died 19 August 1857, widow of Hon. Henry Dawkins. [Old Plantation Estate gravestone, Clarendon, Jamaica]

DAWKINS, HENRY, born 1698, died 30 June 1744, [Old Plantation Estate gravestone, Clarendon, Jamaica]

DAWKINS, JAMES, born 1722, died 16 September 1757. [Old Plantation Estate gravestone, Clarendon, Jamaica]

THE PEOPLE OF JAMAICA, 1655 TO 1855

DAWSON, Reverend JAMES, in St John's, Jamaica, died in Kingston, Jamaica, on 30 June 1851. [GM.ns36.327]

DAWSON, SUSANNA, born 1758, a seamstress from London, to Jamaica via London aboard the Fanny in 1774. [TNA.T47.9/11]

DEANS, RACHEL SUSANNA, widow of Alexander Deans, Master in Chancery of Jamaica, married A. Peyton Phelps in London on 12 May 1835. [GM.ns4.88]

DEBNAM, THOMAS, fought at the Battle of Sedgemoor in Somerset, on 6 July 1685 against the forces of King James II, captured and transported from Portland Road aboard the Jamaican Merchant of London, master Charles Gardiner, bound for Jamaica in 1685.

DE CASERES, JACOB, a Jewish merchant in Jamaica, petitioned the Council for Trade and Plantations in London, on 30 August 1692. [JCTP]

DE CORDOVA, JEOSHUA HISQUIAU, was born in Amsterdam in 1720, in 1755 he became the Haham of Shaar Hashamaim in Kingston, Neve Shalom in Spanish Town, and Neve Zedek in Port Royal, died 1797.

DE JEAN, EULALIE VVE, died 6 September 1842, husband of Elizabeth Heurleloux, she died in Kingston on 23 July 1830. [Spring Path gravestone, Kingston, Jamaica]

DE JLAVILLE, CATHERINE GUILLEAUMEA, born 1758, wife of Francois Gregoire de la Biche, died 12 September 1826. [Spring Path gravestone, Kingston, Jamaica]

DE LA CREE, EDMOND, a surgeon in Jamaica, 1670. [IRO.Deeds.iii.25]

DEHANY, MARY FRAVELL, daughter of George Dehany in Jamaica, married G. H. C. Scott in London on 27 November 1833. [GM.104.102]

THE PEOPLE OF JAMAICA, 1655 TO 1855

DELAP, FRANCIS, Provost Marshal of Jamaica, versus Charles Knowles the Governor, papers, 1754-1758. [Sussex Archaeological Society, RF17.Bundle xviii]

DELAP, ROBERT, Chief Justice of Jamaica, died 20 April 1757. [GM.37.279]

DELAP, ROBERT, an Assemblyman in Jamaica, died 29 January 1768. [GM.38.47]

DE LA ROCHE, MARY ANN, daughter of John De La Roche of Carisbrook Castle, Jamaica, widow of Henry Coote, married Richard Ferris from Bristol, in Cheltenham on 29 April 1852. [GM.ns38.87]

DE LEON, JACOB RODRIGUEZ, overseer of the synagogue in Port Royal in 1686. [Journal of the House of Assembly in Jamaica. i.114]

DE LESSER, AARON, Grandmaster of the York Masons in Jamaica, died in Kingston, Jamaica, in 1813. [GM.83.595]

DE L'ONGRAIS, JANNE PIERRE, born 1777, died 5 December 1822. [Spring Path gravestone, Kingston, Jamaica]

DELMAR, JACOB, in Jamaica, probate, 1790, PCC

DELPRATT, AGNES, born 1774, widow of Samuel Delpratt in Jamaica, died in Old Charlton on 8 September 1850. [GM.ns34.452]

DELPRATT, ELIZABETH, born 1805, died 18 March 1828. [Spring Path, Kingston, gravestone, Jamaica]

DELPRATT, JOSEPH, in Kingston, Jamaica, a covenant, 1796. [Car.2.331]

DELPRATT, SAMUEL, in Kingston, Jamaica, a covenant, 1796. [Car.2.331]

DE MELLA, ISAAC, in Kingston, probate, 1768.

DE MESQUITA, BENJAMIN BUENO, in Jamaica, with his sons Abraham Cohen and Jacob Ulhuo, in 1665. [SPAWI.1665.949]

DE MESQUITA, REBECCA BUENO, in Jamaica, probate, 1798, PCC

DE METRES, JOHN, born 1698, died at Montego Bay in November 1801. [GM.72.181]

DEMPSTER, Captain Edward, died in Jamaica by 1670. [IRO.Deeds.iii.177]

DENNES, EDMOND, born 1694, died 15 June 1745, also his wife Mary Hormsby, born 1699, died 12 November 1764. [Kingston gravestone, Jamaica]

DENNIS, MARY, born 1750, widow of Francis Dennis in Jamaica, died in London on 2 January 1832. [GM.102.92]

DENNIS, Miss, daughter of Francis Dennis in Jamaica, married James Hewitt Massy Dawson, in Ireland on 11 March 1800. [GM.70.282]

DE PASS, ABRAHAM DANIEL, son of Daniel de Pass in London, , married Judith Lazarus, daughter of Abraham Lazarus, in Kingston, Jamaica, on 8 July 1846. [GM.ns26.418]

DE ROBLES, JACOB DAVID, a Jewish merchant in Jamaica, petitioned the Council for Trade and Plantations in London, on 30 August 1692. [JCTP]

DESBOROUGH, GRACE ALICE, infant daughter of Colonel Desborough of the Royal Artillery, died in Gordon Town, Jamaica, on 24 September 1867. [GM.ns3/5.112]

DES DUNES, MARGUERITE, born 1805, died 6 January 1833. [Spring Path gravestone, Kingston, Jamaica]

DE SOUZA, ISAAC RODRIGUEZ, a Jewish merchant in Jamaica, petitioned the Council for Trade and Plantations in London, on 30 August 1692. [JCTP]

DE TORRES, JACOB, a merchant in Jamaica, Jamaica in 1791. [GM.61.1065]

THE PEOPLE OF JAMAICA, 1655 TO 1855

DE VILER, Mrs GRACE, born 1711, died in Jamaica in 1791. [GM.61.1065]

DIAZ, ISAAC FERNANDES, a Jewish merchant in Jamaica, petitioned the Council for Trade and Plantations in London, on 30 August 1692. [JCTP]

DICK, Mrs CAROLINE, born1774, wife of John Dick an attorney at law, died 1 February 1806. [Kingston gravestone, Jamaica]

DICK, WILLIAM, from Jamaica, married Eliza Lane, daughter of Thomas Lane, in London on 5 September 1811. [GM.81.284]

DICKENSON, EDWARD, born 1795 in Whitely Melksham, died 4 July 1849 on passage from Jamaica. [GM.ns32.646]

DICKENSON, GABRIEL, a planter in Jamaica, died 21 October 1779. [GM.49.520]

DIGNUM, CAROLINE REDWAR, widow of Andrew Graham, and daughter of Reverend Lewis Bowerbank, died in Spanish Town, Jamaica, on 29 March 1867. [GM.ns3/3.819]

DISMORE, EDWARD, Deputy Postmaster of Jamaica, a memorial. [JCTP.15.3.1759]

DISMORE, JANE, born 1727, widow of Edward Dismore former Postmaster General of Jamaica, died in Kingston, Jamaica, on 28 August 1818. [GM.88.379]

DISTIN, MARY CATHERINE, daughter of Henry Distin in Jamaica, married Francis Hamilton from Kensworth, Hertfordshire, in London on 17 March 1840. [GM.ns.13.535]

DOBIE, WILLIAM D., died in Falmouth, Jamaica, on 8 December 1819. [GM.90.186]

DOLLAR, JAMES, born 1800, a merchant, died 6 July 1829. [Kingston gravestone, Jamaica]

THE PEOPLE OF JAMAICA, 1655 TO 1855

DOMAN, NICHOLAS, of Greenvale Pen, Jamaica, died in Trelawney, Jamaica, on 13 April 1829. [GM.99.943]

DOMAN, WEBB, a merchant, died in Falmouth, Jamaica, in 1812. [GM.82.193]

DONNE, ELIZABETH, widow of Reverend Theophilius Donne in Clarendon, Jamaica, died in Bromley, Kent, on 17 February 1859. [GM.ns2/6.438]

DONNE, Reverend THEOPHILIUS, died in Clarendon, Jamaica, on 18 January 1823. [GM.93.379]

DOUCE, WILLIAM, born 1718, son of John and Elizabeth Douce, died 27 May 1720. [Chapleton gravestone, Clarendon, Jamaica]

DOUGLAS, J. G., of Jamaica, was granted Danish citizenship in 1864 by Louis Rothe, Vice Governor of the Danish Virgin Islands. [NLS.Charles Steuart papers, Ch.4019]

DOUGLAS, SAMUEL, an American Loyalist, probably from South Carolina, who was granted land in St Elizabeth parish, Jamaica, in 1782. [TNA]

DOW, ..., on Dow's Estate, a planter of 60 acres in St Andrew's parish in 1754. [TNA.CO137/28/171-196]

DOWNER, Mrs, wife of Colonel Downer in Portland, Jamaica, died in London on 27 September 1800. [GM.70.1110]

DOWNES, ANTHONY, died aboard the King David when bound for Jamaica, probate, 1692, PCC

DOWNES, JAMES, a merchant on High Street, Port Royal, died in 1674. [Jamaica Archives, inventory, liber i]

DOWNIE, JOHN, an American Loyalist, probably from South Carolina, who was granted land in St Elizabeth parish, Jamaica, in 1782. [TNA]

DOWNIE, J., in Clarendon, Jamaica, died 14 December 1812. [GM.83.386]

DOYLEY, Colonel EDWARD, in Jamaica, a letter, 1657. [Bodleian.Rawlinson ms A49]; born 1617, Governor of Jamaica, journal 1655-1662, died 1675. [British Library.Add.ms12433]

DREW, WILLLIAM, of Jamaica, probate, 1657, PCC

DRINKWATER, JOHN, born 1672, died 10 June 1745. [Kingston gravestone, Jamaica]

DRUMMOND, Dr JOHN, died in Westmoreland, Jamaica, on 14 August 1804. [GM.74.690]

DRURY, CHARLES, born 1800, son of Admiral Drury, and Jamaica in 1822. [GM.92.574]

DRURY, Mrs, born 1760, widow of Admiral Thomas Drury, and aunt of Captain Augustus Vere Drury, Royal Navy, died in Kingston, Jamaica, on 20 December 1845. [GM.ns25.558]

DRYSDALE, CATHERINE, born 1758, died 10 August 1794. . [Spring Path, Kingston, gravestone, Jamaica]

DRYSDALE, Mrs EMILE CATHERINE, wife of Henry Drysdale, born 1818, died 27 January 1842. [Spring Path, Kingston, gravestone, Jamaica]

DUANY, EDMUND, a planter in Jamaica, died 24 November 1776. [GM.46.579]

DUNCAN, Mrs, widow of James Duncan, married E. Tovey, from Somerset. In Jamaica on 4 January 1817. [GM.87.12]

DUNCOMB, ELEANOR, born 1749, daughter of John and Elizabeth Winter of Watchet, Smerset, England, and wife of David Duncombe, died 7 September 1786. [St Andrew's gravestone, Jamaica]

THE PEOPLE OF JAMAICA, 1655 TO 1855

DUNKERLEY, Mrs, born 1772, wife of James Dunkerley in Kingston, Jamaica, died in Surrey on 1 November 1801. [GM.71.1061]

DUNKLEY, SUSANNAH MACKENZIE, in Clarendon, Jamaica, married George Atkinson, the Secretary of Jamaica, in Clarendon in 1794. [GM.64.956]

DUNN, SARAH, born 1772, widow of Thomas Dunn in Jamaica, died in Crediton, Devon, on 15 February 1849. [GM.ns31.329]

DUNSTONE, JAMES, Assemblyman and Custos for Trelawney, Jamaica, died there on 12 April 1853. [GM.ns40.97]

DURNING, JOHN, planter of Dromilly Estate, Jamaica, died 14 September 1794. [GM.64.150]

DU ROCHER, MARIE ANGELIQUE, born 1809, died in Kingston on 13 May 1833. [Spring Path gravestone, Kingston, Jamaica]

D'WARRIS, FORTUNATUS, MD, Custos of St George's, died in Jamaica in 1790. [GM.60.476]

D'WARRIS, WILLIAM, born 1752, of Golden Grove, St George's, Jamaica, died in Stanmore on 4 October 1813. [GM.83.505]

DWYER, FRANCIS, a merchant in Jamaica, brother of James Dwer in Bristol, died at Martha Brae, Jamaica, on 2 December 1806. [GM.77.179]

DYAL, MARY, born 1752, a servant from London, bound via London aboard the St James to Jamaica in 1775. [TNA.T47.9/11]

DYER, WILLIAM, former editor of 'The Jamaica Courier', son of Robert Dyer a merchant in Bristol, died in Falmouth, Jamaica, on 26 November 1843. [GM.ns21.223]

DYKES, Captain FRANCIS, from Wapping, London, died in Jamaica, probate, 1691, PCC

DYSON, Captain GEORGE, of the Royal Engineers, born 12 March 1783 in Winchester, died at Spanish Town on 26 June 1806. [St Catherine's gravestone, Jamaica]

EARLSMAN, EDWARD, born 1744, a bookkeeper from London, , via London aboard the Nancy bound for Jamaica in 1774. [TNA.T47.9/11]

EAST, HINTON, Receiver General, Public Treasurer, Judge Advocate, and General of Militia, died in Liguana, Jamaica, in January 1792. [GM.62.279]

EAST, HINTON, born 1784 in Jamaica, son of Edward East, died in St Andrew's, Jamaica, on 14 January 1866. [GM.ns.3/1.595]

EAST, ISABELLA ANNA, daughter of Hinton East, a Councillor of Jamaica, niece of Sir Edward Hyde East, married Oscar Marescaux of the Colonial Bank, son of Adolphe Marescaux in St Omer, France, at Woodford, Jamaica, on 16 March 1864. [GM.ns2/16.650]

EASTERBY, Dr JOHN, died in Jamaica in 1790. [GM.60.1214]

EASTMOND, JAMES, from Lympston, Devon, died on the ship Arms of Holland, in Jamaica, probate 1676, PCC

EASTRIDGE, THOMAS, died in Jamaica, admin., 1659, PCC

EDGER, EDWARD, minister of the Marston Moor at Jamaica, probate 1655, PCC

EDGAR, JOHN, born 1783, son of Preston and Rebecca Edgar of Bristol, died 16 May 1805. [Falmouth gravestone, Jamaica]

EDGAR, Mrs, widow of Dr Handasyde Edgar in Jamaica, died in London on 13 July 1819. [GM.89.93]

EDSOR, JOHN, born 1707, a merchant in Port Royal, died 30 October 1745. [Kingston gravestone, Jamaica]

THE PEOPLE OF JAMAICA, 1655 TO 1855

EDWARDS, BRIAN, born 1807, magistrate in Westmoreland, Jamaica, died there on 13 November 1835. [GM.ns55.335]

EDWARDS, ..., born 1776, son of Bryan Edwards in Jamaica, died at Winchester College on 9 March 1794. [GM.64.264]

EDWARDS, NATHANIEL, born 1750, died 28 January 1771. [St Andrew's gravestone, Jamaica]

EDWARDS, THOMAS, from Tudham, Suffolk, died in Jamaica, admin., 1656, PCC

EDWARDS, WILLIAM, fought at the Battle of Sedgemoor in Somerset, on 6 July 1685 against the forces of King James II, captured and transported from Portland Road aboard the Jamaican Merchant of London, master Charles Gardiner, bound for Jamaica in 1685.

EDWARDES, JOHN PUSEY, of Pusey Hall, Jamaica, died in London on 30 May 1822. [GM.92.572]

EFFINGHAM, Countess, wife of the Earl of Effingham the Governor of Jamaica, died on passage from Jamaica to New York on 14 October 1791, and was buried in Spanish Town, Jamaica. [GM.61.1234]

EGAN, FRANCIS, from Jamaica, died in London on 30 July 1849. [GM.ns32.327]

ELBRIDGE, ..., Jamaican estate papers, 1744-1800. [Bristol Record Office. Ac/wo/10]

ELKEN, GEORGE, a gentleman from Stepney, London, died in Jamaica, probate, 1687, PCC

ELKINS, ISAAC, a butcher in Port Royal, 1672. [IRO.Deeds.V.248]

ELLETSON, GOODIN, from Jamaica, died in North Carolina on 10 November 1789. [GM.60.179]

ELLETSON, ROGER HOPE, Governor of Jamaica, married Miss Gamon, in London on 17 April 1770. [GM.47.190]; he died on 29 November 1775. [GM.45.607]

ELLETSON, Mrs, born 1779, wife of Roger Hope Elletson the Lieutenant Governor of Jamaica, died 1767. [GM.37.279]

ELLETSON, THOMAS HOPE, of Hope Plantation, parish of St Andrew, Jamaica. [JCTP.14.3.1754]

ELLIOT, MATTHEW, fought at the Battle of Sedgemoor in Somerset, on 6 July 1685 against the forces of King James II, captured and transported from Portland Road aboard the Jamaican Merchant of London, master Charles Gardiner, bound for Jamaica in 1685.

ELLIS, WILLIAM B., an attorney and Assemblyman for Portland, died in Spanish Town, Jamaica, in June 1795. [GM.65.791]

ELLISON, ROBERT, a Lieutenant of the 60th Rifles, died 1843. [Falmouth gravestone, Jamaica]

ELLISTON, Mrs, born 1725, a lady from London, emigrating via Portsmouth aboard the Judith and Hilaria bound for Jamaica in 1776. [TNA.T47.9/11]

ELMES, H. L., born 1815, son of James Elmes at the Port of London, a surveyor and architect, died in Jamaica on 20 November1847. [GM.ns29.21]

ELMSLIE, JOHN, from Jamaica, died in Windsor on 23 July 1829. [GM.99.188]

ENGLISH, ALEXANDER, born 1753 from London, bound via London aboard the Fanny for Jamaica in 1774. [TNA.T47.9/11]

ENGLEFIELD, Captain EPSLEY, in Honey Lane, Port Royal, 1660s. [IRO.Deeds.iii.77]

ENRIQUES, JACOB JEOSA BUENO, a Jamaican, petitioned King Charles II for a licence to work a copper mine in Jamaica, and to use Jewish law and hold synagogues, 1661. [SPAWI.1661.138]

ENRIQUES, JOSEF BUENO, a Jamaican, petitioned King Charles II for authority to use Jewish law and hold synagogues, 1661. [SPAWI.1661.138]

ENRIQUES, MOISE BUENO, a Jamaican, petitioned King Charles II in 1661. [SPAWI.1661.138]

ERGAS, RALPH, died in Kingston, Jamaica, on 20 March 1782. [GM.52.206]

ERGESAGED, R., born 1755, a clerk from London, via London aboard the Great Marlow bound for Jamaica in 1774. [TNA.T47.9/11]

ESPINOSA, ABRAHAM, a merchant in Jamaica, was granted denization on 3 July 1671. [Patent Roll, 23 Car ii part 5]

ESCOUGH, NATHANIEL, a doctor and physician in Jamaica in 1674. [IRO.I.206]

ETHERIDGE, JAMES, born 1814, son of Thomas Etheridge of Sibtonhall, Suffolk, died in Jamaica on 14 December1853. [GM.ns41.439]

ETHERIDGE, THOMAS, born 1772, son of Reverend Robert Etheridge in Starston, Suffolk, died in Port Royal, Jamaica, on 23 March 1797. [GM.67.528]

EVANS, Mrs MARY MARTIN, from Kingston, Jamaica, died in Buckinghamshire on 12 December 1812. [GM.82.672]

EVES, EDWARD, fought at the Battle of Sedgemoor in Somerset, on 6 July 1685 against the forces of King James II, captured and transported from Portland Road aboard the Jamaican Merchant of London, master Charles Gardiner, bound for Jamaica in 1685.

EWING, JOHN, a merchant from London, died in Jamaica, probate, 1686, PCC

EYCOTT, WILLIAM, born 1744, with his wife, from Gloucestershire, bound from Bristol to Jamaica in 1774. [TNA.T47.9/11]

EYRE, ..., son of Lieutenant Governor Eyre, was born in Kingshouse, Spanish Town, Jamaica, on 5 February 1863. [GM.ns2/14.512]; also, a daughter born 22 December 1865 in Flamstead, Jamaica. [GM.ns3/1.416]

FAIRLIE, JAMES, a merchant in Warwick, Virginia, before 1776, later in Pensacola, West Florida, afterwards in Kingston, Jamaica, by 1789. [TNA.AO13.34.478]; from Kingston, Jamaica, died in Bellfield on 19 May 1819. [GM.88.586]

FALKNER, THOMAS, from Plymouth, died in Jamaica, admin., 1656, PCC

FANNIN, JAMES, from Montego Bay, died in London on 12 June 1808. [GM.78.565]

FANSHAWE, CHARLES GASCOYNE, son of John G. Fanshawe in Parloe, Essex, died in Jamaica in 1801. [GM.71.187]

FARQUHARSON, ANNA, daughter of Charles Farquharson, married Reverend George Augustus Addison from Manchester, in Clarendon, Jamaica, on 4 February 1851. [GM.ns35.545]

FARQUHARSON, ELIZABETH FRANCES, daughter of Matthew Farquharson in St Elizabeth's, Jamaica, married Robert Henry Robertson, son of Duncan Robertson in St Elizabeth's, Jamaica, in London on 19 March 1864. [GM.ns2/16.521]

FARQUHARSON, THOMAS, in Jamaica, a deed, 9 July 1774. [NRS.RD2.216.923]

FAWCETT, GEORGE, in Vere, Jamaica, probate 1685, PCC

THE PEOPLE OF JAMAICA, 1655 TO 1855

FEAKE, JOSHUA, born 1651, died 1684. [St Catherine's gravestone, Jamaica]

FEARON, THOMAS PETERS, from Jamaica, married Anna Maria Boyfield from Lee, Kent, on 2 March 1782. [GM.52.149]

FENN, ANDREW, died in Jamaica in 1790. [GM.60.766]

FENWICK, HENRY, a gentleman in St Katherine's, Jamaica, 1673, [IRO.Deeds.i.147]; probate, 1695, PCC

FERGUSON, ELIZABETH, born 1757, from London, bound via London aboard the Royal Charlotte for Jamaica in 1774. [TNA.T47.9/11]

FERGUSON, EUPHEMIA, born 1758, from London, bound via London aboard the Royal Charlotte for Jamaica in 1774. [TNA.T47.9/11]

FERGUSON, JOHN, MD, formerly in Kingston, Jamaica, died in Clapham on 22 July 1856. [GM.ns2/1.391]

FERGUSON, Dr THOMAS, born 1706, died 1791 in Jamaica. [GM.61.1065]

FERNANDES, BENJAMIN DIAS, a merchant in Kingston, Jamaica, an executor in 1769. [ActsPCCol.v.118]; in 1775, [Car 3.155]

FIDLER, Reverend DANIEL, in Westmoreland, Jamaica, headmaster of Manning Free School, died at The Castle, Savanna la Mar, Jamaica, on 11 April 1863. [GM.ns2/14.80]

FIELD, ...daughter of Captain Field of the 6th Regiment, was born in Newcastle, Jamaica, on 16 October 1865. [GM.ns3/1.112]

FINCH, WILLIAM, born 1763, from London, via London aboard the Standlinch bound for Jamaica in 1774. [TNA.T47.9/11]

FINLAYSON, JOHN, an American Loyalist, probably from South Carolina, who was granted land in St Elizabeth parish in 1782. [TNA]

FINNEMORE, JOHN, fought at the Battle of Sedgemoor in Somerset, on 6 July 1685 against the forces of King James II, captured and transported from Portland Road aboard the Jamaican Merchant of London, master Charles Gardiner, bound for Jamaica in 1685.

FINNIAN, ROBERT, from Jamaica, died in Clifton on 15 September 1800. [GM.70.1107]

FISHER, JOHN, a cabinet maker in Charleston, South Carolina, a Loyalist who moved to Kingston, Jamaica, in 1783. [TNA.AO12.51.256]; born 1737, died in Kingston on 1 November 1804. [Kingston gravestone, Jamaica]

FLANAGAN, Dr WILLIAM, died in Kingston, Jamaica, in 1793. [GM.63.1152]

FLEMING, JOHN, a merchant in Port Royal, Jamaica, probate, 1692, PCC

FLETCHALL, THOMAS, in 96 District, South Carolina, a Loyalist soldier in S.C., moved to Montego Bay, Jamaica, in 1780. [TNA.AO12.52.127]

FLETCHER, ALEXANDER, a tailor in Port Royal, Jamaica,1670. [IRO.Deeds.iii,33]

FLETCHER, ELIZABETH, born 1690 in Jamaica, widow of Jacob Fletcher of Whitehall Estate, St Anne's, Jamaica, died at Gay's Hill, Jamaica, on 1 February 1810. [GM.80.384]

FLETCHER, JOHN, born 1759, from Hull, via Hull aboard the Jamaica Packet bound for Jamaica in 1774. [TNA.T47.9/11]

FLOWER, ROGER, a baker from Covent Garden, London, later in St Katherine's parish, Jamaica, died there, probate, 1689, PCC

FLUELLIN, LEONARD, in Jamaica, 7 June 1689. [TNA.Prob.4/24250]

FONOLL, GASPAR CAMP, born in Spain on 6 January 1776, died 31 January 1829. [Spring Path, Kingston, gravestone, Jamaica]

FONSECA, ISAAC DA SILVA, probate, 25 August 1766

FONSECA, JACOB, in Jamaica, probate, 1740, PCC

FONSECA, RACHEL, in Jamaica, probate, 1807, PCC

FOORD, EDWARD, was appointed a Member of the Council of Jamaica. [JTP;7.5.1776]; died in Kingston, Jamaica, in 1776. [GM.47.295]; a merchant in Kingston, Jamaica, died 13 March 1777. [St Andrew's gravestone, Jamaica]

FOOT, GEORGE FORRESTER, born 1799, died in Clarendon, Jamaica, on 4 December 1820. [GM.91.475]

FOOT, RICHARD, born 1780, a surgeon, died 1802 in Jamaica. [GM.72.785]

FORBES, ALEXANDER, of Jamaica, died on passage to England in 1803. [GM.73.1254]

FORBES, MUNGO, from Jamaica, died in Bristol on 6 April 1807. [GM.77.489]

FORD, GILBERT, the Attorney General of Jamaica, died on 29 January 1768. [GM.38.47]

FORREST, THOMAS, a merchant, late in Jamaica, died in Colchester, Essex, probate, 1682, PCC

FORSTER, GEORGE, born 1763 from Bedford, bound via London aboard the Catharine for Jamaica in 1774. [TNA.T47.9/11]

FORSTER, HENRY, born 1762 from Bedford, bound via London aboard the Catherine for Jamaica in 1774. [TNA.T47.9/11]

FORSTER, JOHN, born 1747, from Jamaica, died in London on 25 December 1840. [GM.ns15.216]

FORSYTH, WILLIAM, born 1757, a husbandman from Surrey, bound via London aboard the Royal Charlotte for Jamaica in 1774. [TNA.T47.9/11]

FOSSETT, ROBERT, from Bedminster, Somerset, died in Jamaica, admin., PCC

FOSTER, ALICE JANE, born 1844, daughter of William Foster, died in Mandeville, Jamaica, on 29 August 1848. [GM.ns30.670]

FOSTER, ARCHIBALD, died 1791 in Jamaica. [GM.61.186]

FOSTER, JOHN, son of Charles Foster in Lancaster, Jamaica, died in Sacramento, California, on 16 October 1849. [GM.ns33.342]

FOSTER, WILLIAM, died in Mandeville, Jamaica, on 7 September 1848. [GM.ns30.670]

FOTHERINGHAM, JAMES, born 1804, died 25 June 1834. [Kingston gravestone, Jamaica]

FOTHERINGHAM, KEITH, born 1815, died 2 November 1847. [Kingston gravestone, Jamaica]

FOULKES, ARTHUR, from Jamaica, married Louisa Locke Glenie, daughter of Archdeacon Glenie, in London on 15 June 1841. [GM.ns16.201]; son of Arthur Foulkes in Bristol, died in Spanish Town, Jamaica, on 15 July 1842. [GM.ns19.110]

FOWLE, WILLIAM, of Wiltshire Estate, died 6 July 1796. [Montego Bay gravestone, Jamaica]

FOWLER, JOHN, sr., fought at the Battle of Sedgemoor in Somerset, on 6 July 1685 against the forces of King James II, captured and transported from Portland Road aboard the Jamaican Merchant of London, master Charles Gardiner, bound for Jamaica in 1685.

FOWLER, JOHN, jr., fought at the Battle of Sedgemoor in Somerset, on 6 July 1685 against the forces of King James II, captured and transported from Portland Road aboard the Jamaican Merchant of London, master Charles Gardiner, bound for Jamaica in 1685.

FOWLER, RICHARD, born 1749, a merchant, with his wife, born 1751, returning via London aboard the James Daukins for Jamaica in 1774. [TNA.T47.9/11]

FOWLES, Captain JOHN, died 25 October 1782, his wife, Maria, died in February 1783. [Kingston gravestone, Jamaica]

FOXLEY, SAMUEL, from London, a merchant in Port Royal, Jamaica, probate, 1698, PCC

FRANCIS, ELIZABETH, daughter of S. Francis of Newington Estate, Jamaica, married Captain T. Scott of the Royal Marines, in London on 26 October 1837. [GM.ns8.648]

FRANCO, JOSEPH, in Jamaica, probate, 1808, PCC

FRANCO, LEAH, in Jamaica, probate, 1808, PCC

FRANCKEN, HENRY ANDREW, Assistant Judge of Port Royal, Jamaica, died in Kingston, Jamaica, in May 1795. [GM.65.791]

FRANCKLYN, PETER, the Customs Collector at Kingston, Jamaica, married Mrs Elizabeth Harding of Weston Favel Estate, Trelawney, Jamaica, in September 1794. [GM.64.1052]

FRANCKLYN, THOMAS, from Jamaica, died 26 July 1767. [GM.37.524]

FRASER, DONALD, an American Loyalist, probably from South Carolina, who was granted land in St Elizabeth parish in 1782. [TNA]

FREEBAIRN, THOMAS, died in Jamaica in 1790. [GM.60.1214]

FREEMAN, HUMPHREY, born 1628 'who was at the taking of the island', died 6 August 1692. [St Catherine's gravestone, Jamaica]; in Thames Street, Port Royal, in 1659. [BM. Add.mss.12423/80]

FREEMAN, JAMES, died in Jamaica in 1790. [GM.60.1053]

THE PEOPLE OF JAMAICA, 1655 TO 1855

FREEMAN, Lieutenant Colonel MARMADUKE, born 1646, died 1709. [Morant Bay gravestone, Jamaica]

FREEMAN, ROBERT, from Moon, County Kildare, died in Jamaica before April 1674. [Island Record Office, Jamaica, Deeds.liber i.237]

FRENCH, SUSANNAH, born 1744, died 9 September 1818. [Spring Path, Kingston, gravestone, Jamaica]

FRENCH, WILLIAM, from Jamaica, died in London on 14 September 1808. [GM.78.861]

FRENCH, Councillor, died in Kingston, Jamaica, in 1758. [GM.29.45]

FRENCH, Miss, married Captain Stehelin of the Royal Artillery, in Spanish Town, Jamaica, in November 1790. [GM.60.1213]

FROGG, ROBERT, a tailor in Charleston, South Carolina, a Loyalist who moved to Kingston, Jamaica, in 1780. [TNA.AO.12.52.152, etc]

FROST, WILLIAM, in Jamaica, probate, 1681, PCC

FRUSILLA, PHILPOT, born 1747, a bricklayer from London, bound via London aboard the Britannia for Jamaica in 1773. [TNA.T47.9/11]

FRYERS, WILLIAM, born 1744, a clerk from London, via London aboard the Great Marlow bound for Jamaica in 1774. [TNA.T47.9/11]

FUGE, JOHN, born 1687, died in Savanna la Mar, Jamaica, on 9 May 1827. [GM.97.285]

FULLER, JOHN, a planter in Jamaica, accounts, 1719-1728. [Lincoln Archives. Ancaster.9.D.7]

FULLER, ROSE, was appointed Chief Justice of Jamaica in 1753. [Sussex Archaeological Society, Fuller ms]

THE PEOPLE OF JAMAICA, 1655 TO 1855

FURBER, JOHN, fought at the Battle of Sedgemoor in Somerset, on 6 July 1685 against the forces of King James II, captured and transported from Portland Road aboard the Jamaican Merchant of London, master Charles Gardiner, bound for Jamaica in 1685.

FURY, REBECCA, born 1687, died in Falmouth, Jamaica, on 7 April 1827. [GM.97.94]

FYFE, CATHERINE, widow of William Fyfe in Jamaica, died in London on 4 October 1818. [GM.88.473]

FYFE, WILLIAM, died in Kingston, Jamaica, on 6 January 1810. [GM.80.284]

GADES, HARMAN, born 1749, a sugar baker from London, bound via London aboard the Royal Charlotte for Jamaica in 1774. [TNA.T47.9/11]

GABAY, ABRAHAM F. DE IAHACOB, died 1672. [Hunt's Bay gravestone, Jamaica]

GABAY, ABRAHAM DAVID, in Port Royal, 1677. [IRO.Deeds.viii.87]

GAGE, ANN, a victualler in Port Royal, Jamaica, in 1670. [IRO.Deeds.iv.124]

GAINS, ..., daughter of G. E. Gains, surgeon of the 6th Royal Regiment, was born in Newcastle, Jamaica, on 31 May 1864. [GM.ns2/17.231]

GALBRAITH, Reverend EDWARD, of Hanover, Jamaica, died in Lucca, Jamaica, on 19 June 1859. [GM.ns2/9.196]

GALBRAITH, NEIL, an American Loyalist, probably from South Carolina, who was granted land in St Elizabeth parish in 1782. [TNA]

GALBRAITH, Dr, died in Kingston, Jamaica, in 1793. [GM.63.1152]

GALDY, LEWIS, born 1659 in Montpelier, France, a Huguenot refugee, merchant in Port Royal, 'swallowed by the great earthquake of 1692, but survived', died 22 December 1739. [Port Royal gravestone, Jamaica]

GALE, FLORA, born 1672, died in Savanna la Mar, Jamaica, on 7 February 1792. [GM.62.479]

GALE, HENRY, born 19 February 1737, Custos and Colonel of St Elizabeth, died 8 March 1767. [Black River Church gravestone, Jamaica]

GALE, WILLIAM, from Jamaica, died in London on 4 December 1795. [GM.66.1057]

GALLIMORE, JULIA, daughter of J. Gallimore, married Sir John Gordon of Earlston, in Water Valley, Jamaica, in December 1811. [GM.81.585]

GALLIMORE, Miss, daughter of Jarvis Gallimore in Jamaica, married James Scarlet, on 28 July 1791. [GM.61.774]

GALLOP, JAMES, fought at the Battle of Sedgemoor in Somerset, on 6 July 1685 against the forces of King James II, captured and transported from Portland Road aboard the Jamaican Merchant of London, master Charles Gardiner, bound for Jamaica in 1685.

GARDEN, GEORGE W., from Jamaica, married Maria Jane Shannon, daughter of W. C. Shannon in County Clare, in London on 28 October 1845. [GM.ns27.193]

GARDINER, JOHN, fought at the Battle of Sedgemoor in Somerset, on 6 July 1685 against the forces of King James II, captured and transported from Portland Road aboard the Jamaican Merchant of London, master Charles Gardiner, bound for Jamaica in 1685.

GARDINER, ROBERT BARLOW, born 1818, Chief Engineer of Roadsa and Bridges, died in Spanish Town, Jamaica, on 14 June 1859. [GM.ns2/7.314]

GARDINER, THOMAS, in Jamaica, 9 July 1691. [TNA.Prob.4.24661]

THE PEOPLE OF JAMAICA, 1655 TO 1855

GARNETT, JOHN, in Kingston, Jamaica, letters to family in Manchester, 1794-1805. [Lancashire Record Office, DDQ1-30]

GARTH, Miss, daughter of Arthur Garth in Jamaica, married James Jefferies of Staunton Dew, Somerset, in London on 6 September 1796. [GM.66.789]

GASPARD, MARIA LOUISE, born 1728, died 29 July 1818.[Spring Path, Kingston, gravestone, Jamaica]

GAYNER, JAMES, born 1759, died 1796. [Falmouth gravestone, Jamaica]

GAYNOR, JOHN, born 1746, settled in Jamaica in 1760, a magistrate, died in Culloden Estate, St Anne's, Jamaica, on 3 May 1823. [GM.93.478]

GEDDES, ALEXANDER, of Annandale, Jamaica, married Frances Evershed, daughter of Thomas Evershed, Pallingham, Sussex, in London on 22 December 1852. [GM.ns39.305]

GEDDES, Mrs ELEANOR, wife of George Geddes in Woodford Bridge, died in Jamaica on 12 July 1852. [GM.ns38.433]

GEDDES, HELEN JOSEPHINE, daughter of George Geddes, married James Bannatyne Blair, a Lieutenant of the 6th Royal Regiment, at Halfwaytree Church, Jamaica, on 5 October 1865. [GM.ns3/1.117]

GEGG, Reverend HENRY, born 1813, from Trelawney, died at Rookesby Park, St Anne's, Jamaica, on 11 August 1850. [GM.ns33.102]

GEGG, Reverend JOHN HENRY, born 1785, from Uphill, Somerset, died in Jamaica on 11 May 1842. [GM.ns19.215]

GEGG, Reverend JOSEPH, married Maria Louise Levison Doria Gordon, daughter of William Gordon MD, in Jamaica on, 7 January 1847. [GM.ns27.541]

THE PEOPLE OF JAMAICA, 1655 TO 1855

GIBBON, Mrs E., born 1690 in Port Royal, Jamaica, died in Jamaica in 1790. [GM.60.1148]

GIBNEY, WILLIAM AUGUSTUS, born 1823, son of Dr Gibney in Cheltenham, died in Kingston, Jamaica, in 1848. [GM.ns30.110]

GIBSON, Dr ROBERT, died in Belvidere, Hanover, Jamaica, on 4 June 1797. [GM.67.800]

GIDDONS, JAMES, born 1749, a millwright from London, bound via London aboard the Mars for Jamaica in 1774. [TNA.T47.9/11]

GILBERT, WILLIAM, born 1750, , a husbandman from Somerlyton in Suffolk, bound aboard the Norfolk via Yarmouth for Jamaica in 1775. [TNA.T47.9/11]

GILL, HUGH, fought at the Battle of Sedgemoor in Somerset, on 6 July 1685 against the forces of King James II, captured and transported from Portland Road aboard the Jamaican Merchant of London, master Charles Gardiner, bound for Jamaica in 1685.

GILLMAN, WILLIAM, a planter in the parish of St John, Jamaica, probate, 1680, PCC

GILPIN, R., born 1760, a Customs officer in Falmouth, Jamaica, died there on 25 May 1819. [GM.89.88]

GLADSTONE, ALEXANDER, born 1809, from St Elizabeth's, Jamaica, died in Carlisle on 18 August 1856. [GM.ns2/1.521]

GLANVILLE, TRYPHENA, daughter of Samuel Glanville, from Jamaica, married John Slyfield Garland, in Otley St Mary on 28 October 1851. [GM.ns37.84]

GLEED, HENRY, a merchant in Port Royal, a letter, 1672. [IRO.Deeds.i.215]

GODDARD, JAMES, born 1658.son of James Goddard of South Marston, Wiltshire, Secretary to the Governor, died 21 July 1691. [St Catherine's gravestone, Jamaica]

GODDEN, Reverend THOMAS, formerly a Baptist missionary in Spanish Town, Jamaica, died in Bristol on 30 November 1824. [GM.95.187]

GOLD, CHARLES, an indentured servant, from England to Port Royal, Jamaica, aboard the Saint George, Captain James, landed 3 January 1688, and sold for 60 dollars to William Ross the Marshal there. [Taylor ms, Institute of Jamaica]

GOLDSON, THOMAS, in Port Royal, Jamaica, probate, 1784, PCC

GOLDWIN, THOMAS, born 1744, a merchant from London, from London aboard the Lady's Adventure bound for Jamaica in 1776. [TNA.T47.9/11]

GOMERSAL, EZEKIAL, a member of the Council of Jamaica in 1716. [JCTP.1716.14]

GOMEZ, DAVID, a merchant in Port Royal in 1670. [IRO.]

GONSALES, ABRAHAM, a merchant in Kingston, Jamaica, in St Ann's in 1737, [Car.3.155][a petitioner in Jamaica in 1752, [ActsPCCol.1745-1766.151]; in Jamaica, probate, 1760, PCC

GONSALES, ISAAC, in Jamaica, probate, 1764, PCC

GONSALES, JACOB NUNES, died 1729. [Hunts Bay gravestone, Jamaica]

GONSALES, JACOB, a merchant in Kingston, Jamaica, a planter in St Ann's in 1737, [Car.3.155]; a petitioner in Jamaica in 1752, [ActsPCCol.1745-1766.151]; in London in 1775. [Car.3.155]

GOOCH, HENRY, born 1817, son of Henry Gooch in Camberwell, died in Jamaica on 21 May 1845. [GM.ns24.214]

THE PEOPLE OF JAMAICA, 1655 TO 1855

GOODLAD, WILLIAM, fought at the Battle of Sedgemoor in Somerset, on 6 July 1685 against the forces of King James II, was captured and transported from Portland Road aboard the Jamaican Merchant of London, master Charles Gardiner, bound for Jamaica in 1685.

GOODWIN, GEORGE, born 1671, died in Jamaica in April 1776. [GM.46.249]

GORDON, FRANCIS, in Kenmore, Jamaica, brother of Sir James Gordon of Earlston, died in Spanish Town, Jamaica, on 27 July 1823. [GM.93.647]

GORDON, GEORGE W., from Jamaica, married Marie Jane Shannon, daughter of W. T. Shannon in County Clare, in London o 28 October 1846. [GM.ns22.193]

GODON, GEORGE, born 1789, son of John Gordon in Bristol, died in Moorpark, Jamaica, on 23 May 1850. [GM.ns34.454]

GORDON, ROBERT, from Jamaica, died in Windsor on 12 February 1833. [GM.103.187]

GORDON, THOMAS, an American Loyalist, probably from South Carolina, who was granted land in St Elizabeth parish in 1782. [TNA]

GORDON, WILLIAM, a merchant from London, died in Jamaica before November 1673. [IRO.Deeds.I.209]

GOSLING, DANIELL, in Port Royal, Jamaica, probate, 1697, PCC

GOWIE, ALEXANDER, born 1751, a carpenter from London, via London aboard the Great Marlow bound for Jamaica in 1774. [TNA.T47.9/11]

GRADWELL, ROGER, born 1710, from Liverpool, died 15 January 1738. [Kingston gravestone, Jamaica]

GRAHAM, BRICE, born 1783, formerly a merchant in Kingston, Jamaica, died at Latimer's Pen, Jamaica, on 19 May 1849. [GM.ns37.334]

GRAHAM, CHARLES, born 1751, died 9 May 1801. [St Catherine's gravestone, Jamaica]

GRAHAM, JOHN, born 1725, a merchant, died 15 March 1799. [Kingston gravestone, Jamaica]

GRANT, DANIEL, of Maggoty, a planter of 300 acres in St Andrew's parish in 1754. [TNA.CO137/28/171-196]

GRANT, JAMES, an American Loyalist, probably from South Carolina, who was granted land in St Elizabeth parish, Jamaica, in 1782. [TNA]

GRANT, JAMES, an American Loyalist, probably from South Carolina, who was granted land in St Elizabeth parish, Jamaica, in 1782. [TNA]

GRANT, JOHN, an American Loyalist, probably from South Carolina, who was granted land in St Elizabeth parish, Jamaica, in 1782. [TNA]

GRAHAM, JAMES F., Assemblyman for St Thomas in the Vale, Jamaica, died in Villa Pen, Spanish Town, Jamaica, on 1 February 1820. [GM.90.281]

GRAHAM, THOMAS, an American Loyalist, probably from South Carolina, who was granted land in St Elizabeth parish, Jamaica, in 1782. [TNA]

GRAHAM-CLARK, family, in Jamaica, papers, 1820-1858. [Gloucester Record Office, D1889]

GRANT, MARY, born circa 1810 in Kingston, Jamaica, she married Mr Seacole an English merchant on 10 November 1836, owner of a lodging house -Blundell Hall in Kingston, a nurse in Jamaica and in Panama, later in England, died in October 1881. [JHR.XVII]

GRAY, JOHN, born 1749, a gentleman, with his wife Sarah, born 1749, from London, bound via London aboard the West Indian for Jamaica in 1774. [TNA.T47.9/11]43.218]

GRAY, JOHN W., in Port Maria, Jamaica, died 1854. [GM.ns43.218]

GRAY, ROBERT, an American Loyalist, an indigo planter from Canefield, Cheraw District, South Carolina, moved to Jamaica and was granted land in St Elizabeth parish, Jamaica, in 1782. [TNA.AO13.9, 8.237-249]

GRAY, THOMAS JOSEPH, from Jamaica, graduated MD from Edinburgh University in 1802. [EMG.33]

GRAY, WILLIAM, late Provost Marshal of Jamaica and Assemblyman for Port Royal, died in Jamaica in April 1788. [GM.58.658]

GREEN, W., died 1812 in Jamaica. [GM.82.603]

GREGORY, ARTHUR, a planter of 160 acres in St Andrew's parish, Jamaica, in 1754. [TNA.CO137/28/171-196]

GREGORY, JOHN, a Councillor of Jamaica. [JCTP; 11.7.1759]

GREGORY, MATTHEW, born 1693, a physician, died 31 December 1779, his wife Lucretia born 1707, died 29 January 1750. [St Catherine's gravestone, Jamaica]

GREGORY, MATTHEW, sr., born 1665, died 6 September 1715. [St Catherine's gravestone, Jamaica]

GREGORY, M., in St Catherine's, Jamaica, will, 1778. [BM.Add.ch.17266]

GREGSON, NICHOLAS, in Aldgate, London, late of Jamaica, probate, 1693, PCC

THE PEOPLE OF JAMAICA, 1655 TO 1855

GRICE, RICHARD, a citizen and merchant tailor of London and Jamaica, probate, 1689, PCC

GRIEVELY, RICHARD, born 1727, from Sussex, a planter returning to Jamaica via London aboard the Hope in 1774. [TNA.T47.9/11]

GRIFFIN, THOMAS, master of the slaver Mary Anne voyaging between Gambia and Jamaica, letters from Jamaica, 1725 to 1729. [Hampshire Record Office, 8M57]

GRIFFIN, SOLOMON, died in Jamaica, admin., 1656, PCC

GRIFFITHS, Reverend GRIFFITH, Rector of Trelawney, died 1815. [Falmouth gravestone, Jamaica]

GRIFFITHS, JOHN, born 1748, a gentleman from Bath, bound to Jamaica via Bristol aboard the Hector in 1775. [TNA.T47.9/11]

GROSETT, MARY HENRIETTA, daughter of John Rock Grosett late of Lacock Abbey, Wiltshire, died in Petersfield, Jamaica on 31 January 1833. [GM.103.479]

GROSETT, WALTER R., died in St George's, Jamaica, in 1824. [GM.94.382]

GUION, JOANES, born 1774 in Curacao, died 1 June 1827. [Spring Path, Kingston, Jamaica, gravestone]

GULSTON, Mrs, widow of Joseph Gulston, and sister of Reverend Woodham, in St Catherine's, Jamaica, died 20 November 1806. [GM.77.179]

GUSSEN, RICHARD, born 1802, settled in Jamaica in 1820, a Privy Councillor, died 8 August 1860. [St Andrew's gravestone, Jamaica]

GUTIEREZ, ISAAC MENDEZ, a Jewish merchant in Jamaica, petitioned the Council for Trade and Plantations in London, on 30 August 1692. [JCTP]

GUTTUREZ, JACOB MENDEZ, a merchant in Jamaica, a petition, 1739, [ActsPCCol.3.644]; in Jamaica, probate, 1752, PCC

GUTTEREZ, MOSES, deceased, his widow Judica and sons Jacob and Joseph Gutterez, daughters Sarah and Leah deceased, all in Jamaica, a petition, 1739. [ActsPCCol.3.644]

GUTIERES, RACHEL GOMES, in Jamaica, probate, 1735, PCC

GUTTUREZ, SARAH, daughter of Moses Gutterez and wife of William Forbes in Jamaica, grand-daughter of Leah Gutterez in 1739. [ActsPCCol.3.644]

GWILLIMS, GWILLIM, a comb-maker from London, died aboard the Mediterranean at Jamaica, probate, 1692, PCC

GWIN, A., with his wife and six servants from Lancashire, bound via Liverpool aboard the John for Jamaica in 1775. [TNA.T47.9/11]

HAFFIE, ..., died in Jamaica on 22 January 1753. [GM.23.51]

HAGAN, BRIANT, died in Jamaica, admin., 1656, PCC

HAGUE, Reverend D. G., a Moravian missionary, died in Jamaica in 1825. [GM.95.479]

HALDANE, GEORGE, Governor of Jamaica, a letter. [JCTP; 23.4.1759]; letter re trade with the enemy, identifies ships and skippers, 2 June 1759. [APCCol.513]; died 26 July 1759. [GM.29.497]

HALL, ANN, daughter of Thomas Dehany Hall in Kingston, Jamaica, died in London on 17 October 1859. [GM.ns277.654]

HALL, Reverend CLARENCE, in St Dorothy's, Jamaica, son of Captain Edward Hall, Royal Navy, died in Marlie, Jamaica, on 23 August 1867. [GM.ns3/2.682]

THE PEOPLE OF JAMAICA, 1655 TO 1855

HALL, Mrs ELIZABETH, born 1766, died 17 November 1807. [Spring Path gravestone, Kingston, Jamaica]

HALL, JAMES, from Jamaica, married Elizabeth, daughter of Lord L'isle in Dawlish, Devon, in 1800. [GM.70.1284]

HALL, JASPER, died in Jamaica on 24 November 1796. [GM.67.262]

HALL, MARY, born 1723, daughter of William Hall in Westmoreland, died 25 July 1735. [St Catherine's gravestone], Jamaica]

HALL, SUSANNAH, daughter of William Hall in Kingston, Jamaica, married James Henry, Assemblyman for St James's, Jamaica, in1801. [GM.71.763]

HALL, WILLIAM, born 1758, a clerk from London, via London aboard the Lady Tuliana bound for Jamaica in 1774. [TNA.T47.9/11]

HALL, WILLIAM JAMES, a Councillor, died in Jamaica on 18 December 1827. [GM.98.286]

HALL, Mr, formerly a singer at Covent Garden, London, died at Morant Bay, Jamaica, in June 1817. [GM.87.184]

HALL, Mrs, born 1751, widow of William Hall in Jamaica, died in Bury St Edmonds, Suffolk, on 30 December 1842. [GM.ns.19.221]

HALLIBURTON, GAVIN, a planter of 130 acres in St Andrew's parish, Jamaica, in 1754. [TNA.CO137/28/171-196]

HALS, Major THOMAS, born 1632, died 27 February 1701. [Halse Hall gravestone, Jamaica]

HALSE, THOMAS, born 1675, died 27 August 1702. [Halse Hall gravestone, Jamaica]

HALSE, THOMAS, born 1699, died20 November 1737. [Halse Hall gravestone, Jamaica]

THE PEOPLE OF JAMAICA, 1655 TO 1855

HAMILTON, Lord ARCHIBALD, Governor of Jamaica, 1710-1716, papers 1711-1715. [Bodleian Library.Rawlinson.A312]

HAMILTON, CHENEY, the Receiver General and Public Treasurer of Jamaica, died in Kingston, Jamaica, on 17January 1820. [GM.90.377]

HAMILTON, Reverend EDWARD MONTAGUE, son of Cheney Hamilton in Jamaica, married Susan Carne, daughter of John Carne of Falmouth, in Stoke Damerel on 17 April 1844. [GM.ns21.645]

HAMILTON, PETER, an American Loyalist, probably from South Carolina, who was granted land in St Elizabeth parish, Jamaica, in 1782. [TNA]

HAMILTON, ROBERT, of Vineyard Pen, Jamaica, Colonel of the Kingston Militia, and Magistrate of St Andrew's, Jamaica, died in 1814. [GM.84.187]

HAMILTON, THOMAS, a surgeon from Shadwell, Middlesex, died aboard the Adventure at Jamaica, probate, 1693, PCC

HAMILTON, Mr, died in Jamaica in October 1792. [GM.62.1220]

HAMIT, HENRY, fought at the Battle of Sedgemoor in Somerset, on 6 July 1685 against the forces of King James II, captured and transported from Portland Road aboard the Jamaican Merchant of London, master Charles Gardiner, bound for Jamaica in 1685.

HAMMOND, GEORGE, from Jamaica, married Miss Berthon in London on 6 August 1793. [GM.63.859]

HAMMOND, JAMES, a merchant in Kingston, Jamaica, died 25 August 1812. [GM.82.670]

HAMMOND, WILLIAM, son of William Hammond a solicitor in Ipswich, died at sea off Jamaica in 1820. [GM.90.188]

THE PEOPLE OF JAMAICA, 1655 TO 1855

HAMPSON, Sir GEORGE FRANCIS, in Jamaica, died 24 December 1774. [GM.45.46]

HANCE, JAMES, of Jamaica, died on board the John bound for Jamaica in 1812. [GM.82.193]; a merchant, born 1769, died 23 May 1812. [Kingston gravestone, Jamaica]

HANDASYDE, Colonel THOMAS, Governor of Jamaica, 1703.

HANDFIELD, GEORGE J., born 1824, son of Captain Handfield, Royal Navy, grandson of Colonel Handfield the Commissary General of Ireland, great grandson of Colonel John Handfield the Governor of Fort Pitt in Canada, Archdeacon, died in Spanish Town, Jamaica on 3 February 1864. [GM.ns2/16.533]

HANNAFORD, ELIZA GAY, daughter of Stephen Hannaford, married William Tabois Smith, in Jamaica on 7 April 1836. [GM.ns26.528]

HANSBROW, HENRY, died in Kingston, Jamaica, in 1796. [GM.66.618]

HANSON, FRANCIS, an armiger, from Coventry, Warwickshire, died in Port Royal, Jamaica, probate, 1692, 1697, PCC

HAMSON, WILLIAM, a blacksmith in Port Royal in 1679. [IRO.Deeds.x.224]

HANSON, Miss, daughter of John Hanson in Jamaica, married Lieutenant Colonel Blake of the 20th Light Dragoons, in Hampton in 1814. [GM.84.392]

HARBOTTLE, WILLIAM, died in Jamaica in 1791. [GM.61.682]

HARDING, BERNARD, from Jamaica, graduated MD from Edinburgh University in 1796. [EMG.27]

HARDING, Mrs ELIZABETH, of Weston Favel Estate, Jamaica, married Peter Francklyn the Customs Collector of Kingston, Jamaica, there in September 1794. [GM.64.1952]

THE PEOPLE OF JAMAICA, 1655 TO 1855

HARDING, JAMES, a merchant in Jamaica in 1672/1673. [IRO.I.114/208]

HARDSON, ROBERT, a surgeon in Port Royal, 1679. [IRO.Deeds. iii.244]

HARDY, FRANCIS, died 12 February 1733. [Kingston gravestone, Jamaica]

HARDY, GEORGE, born 1779, died 31 October 1831. [Spring Path gravestone, Kingston, Jamaica]

HARRIS, ED., born 1666, died 4 July 1723, husband of Elizabeth – daughter of William and Emma Webb in St Dorothy's – died 30 May 1692, parents of Elizabeth, 163-1693. [St John's gravestone, Jamaica]

HARRIS, JOHN WALLACE, born 1804, Clerk of the Peace, died 15 October 1857. [St Andrew's gravestone, Jamaica]

HARRIS, JOSEPH, born 1718, late of Kingston, died 6 July 1760. . [Kingston gravestone, Jamaica]

HARRIS, THOMAS, died 1718. [St Andrew's gravestone, Jamaica]

HARRIS, WILLIAM FORTESCUE, Major of the Port Royal Militia, died in Kingston, Jamaica, in July 1793. [GM.63.862]

HARRISON, CHRISTOPHER, son of T. Harrison, Attorney General, died in Jamaica on 11 December 1811. [GM.82.488]

HARRISON, DOROTHY, daughter of Thomas Harrison the Attorney General of Jamaica, married Edmund Bullock of Jamaica, in Bath in 1796. [GM.66.789]

HARRISON, EDWARD, born 1654, died 29 August 1695, [St Andrew's gravestone, Jamaica]

THE PEOPLE OF JAMAICA, 1655 TO 1855

HARRISON, EDWARD STAINES, from Scarborough, Yorkshire, a Lieutenant of the 1st West Indian Regiment, died 13 September 1856. [St Andrew's gravestone, Jamaica]

HARRISON, JOHN, from London, died in Kingston, Jamaica, in 1799. [GM.69.624]

HARRISON, M. in Jamaica, a letter, 1656. [Bodleian, Rawlinson.A43.111]

HARRISON, MARGARET A., daughter of Thomas Harrison the Attorney General of Jamaica, married Henry Veitch in Madeira in 1808. [GM.78.1187]

HARRISON, THOMAS, HM Attorney General of Jamaica, son of Sir T. Harrison the Chamberlain of London, brother of Benjamin Harrison, treasurer of Christ's Hospital, died in Spanish Town, Jamaica, on 12 February 1792. [GM.62.279]

HART, WILLIAM, born 1752, a labourer from London emigrating via London aboard the William and Mary bound for Jamaica in 1774. [TNA.T47.9/11]

HARVEY, WILLIAM, from Aldgate, London, died in Jamaica, probate, 1692, PCC

HARWOOD, JOHN, a surgeon from Whitechapel, London, died in Jamaica, probate,1693, PCC

HASWELL, Reverend WILLIAM JEPSON, born 1779, late of Corpus Christi College, Oxford, chaplain to HMS Pique died in St John's rectory, Jamaica, on 9 August 1817. [GM.87.561]

HATHAWAY, SILAS, born 1751, from Jamaica, died in London on 9 September 1826. [GM.96.284]

HATON, ROBERT, jr., a merchant in Port Royal, Jamaica, probate, 1687, PCC

THE PEOPLE OF JAMAICA, 1655 TO 1855

HAUGHTON, SAMUEL WILLIAMS, Speaker of the Jamaica Assembly, died in Westmoreland, Jamaica, on 12 August 1793. [GM.63.1051]

HAWORTH, JOHN SMITH, son of Joshua Haworth in Hull, died in Savanna-la-Mar, Jamaica, in January 1802. [GM.72.374]

HAY, JAMES, born 1696, a judge of the Grand Court, died 7 October 1735. [St Catherine's gravestone, Jamaica]

HAY, MICHAEL, in Kingston, Jamaica, died 12 December 1762. [GM.32.241]

HAY, THOMAS, Secretary of Jamaica, died 28 January 1769. [GM.39.110]

HAYLES, JOHN, born 1736, died 5 September 1766. Sheckles Estate, Clarendon, gravestone, Jamaica]

HAYMAN, GEORGE, born 1822, died 25 June 1831. [Spring Path gravestone, Kingston, Jamaica]

HAYNES, JOHN, in Jamaica, died 1758. [GM.28.556]

HAYWOOD, ELIZABETH, born 1679, died in Spanish Town, Jamaica, on 30 October 1809. [GM.79.182]

HEAD, JOHN, a merchant in Jamaica, 1672. [IRO.Deeds.V.1]

HEATH, Dr EMANUEL, Rector of the Anglican church in Port Royal, 1692. [IRO]

HEATHCOTE, brothers, title deeds to property in St Catherine's parish, Jamaica, 1699-1712. [Lincoln Archives. Ancaster 1.B.3]

HELVAR, CARY, born 1633, a merchant, died 5 July 1672. [St Catherine's gravestone, Jamaica]

HEMMING, GEORGE, married Miss Bracebridge from Weddington, in Jamaica on 19 September 1769. [GM.39.462]

THE PEOPLE OF JAMAICA, 1655 TO 1855

HENCKELL, JOHN, born 1750, Chief Judge, died 10 December 1801. [St Catherine's gravestone, Jamaica]; died 4 December 1802. [GM.72.272]

HENDERSON, ALEXANDER, born 1696, Attorney General, died 13 April 1732. [St Catherine's gravestone, Jamaica]

HENDERSON, Mrs ELIZABETH, widow of Benjamin Henderson in St Ann's, Jamaica, died in Bristol on 16 August 1851. [GM.ns36.443]

HENDERSON, JOHN, born 1749, a gentleman from London, bound via London aboard the Royal Charlotte for Jamaica in 1774. [TNA.T47.9/11]

HENRIQUES, A. Q., born 1775, formerly in Jamaica, died in Shirley, Hampshire, on 30 May 1840. [GM.ns14.110]

HENRIQUES, ISAAC, of Port Royal, Jamaica, probate, 1722

HENRIQUES, JOSEPH, in Jamaica, probate, 1810, PCC

HENRIQUES, MOSES, a merchant in Kingston, Jamaica, 1819, a witness to David Wolfe's deed. [NRS.RD5.193.713]

HENRY, JAMES, the Assemblyman for St Ann's, Jamaica, married Susannah Hall, daughter of William Hall, in Kingston, Jamaica, in 1801. [GM.ns.71.763]

HENRY, W., born 1806, son of Alexander Henry in Pentonville, died in Jamaica on 17 July 1835. [GM.ns.4.445]

HENSLEY, WILLIAM, born 1734, a gentleman returning via Bristol to Jamaica aboard the Charlotte Peg in 1774. [TNA.T47.11]

HEPBURNE, ROBERT, a mariner from Stepney, London, died in Jamaica, probate, 1692, PCC

HERBERT, THOMAS COTTLE, born 1801, son of R. M. Herbert in Bristol, died in Jamaica on 17 March 1830. [GM.100.651]

THE PEOPLE OF JAMAICA, 1655 TO 1855

HESLOP, ALEXANDER, of the Inner Temple, son of W. Heslop in Jamaica, married Emma Kemp, daughter of Major General Kemp, of East Hothley, Sussex, in London in 1842. [GM.ns18.313]

HEWITT, ELIZABETH, a dealer in Bird's Alley, Port Royal, [IRO.Deeds.xv.57]

HEWITT, WILLIAM KELLIT, from Jamaica, died in London on 11 June 1812. [GM.82.605]

HEY, WILLIAM, the Customs Commissioner, married Miss Paplay, in Jamaica on 5 April 1783. [GM.53.363]

HEYWOOD, PETER, Governor of Jamaica, 21 May 1716.

HIATT, JOHN, born 1722, Chief Justice in St Ann's, Jamaica, died on Mount Plenty, Jamaica, on 14 September 1820. [GM.90.570]

HIBBERT, HENRY ROBERTS, son of George Hibberts in London, died in Kingston, Jamaica, on 14 July 1825. [GM.95.286]

HIBBERT, THOMAS, born 1709 in Manchester, England, son of Robert and Mary Hibbert, settled in Jamaica in 1734, a merchant in Kingston and a plantation owner, died 20 May 1780. [Annotto Bay gravestone, Jamaica]

HICKS, DANIEL, a merchant in Port Royal, Jamaica, probate, 1688, PCC

HICKES, NICHOLAS, a merchant in Port Royal, 1670/1673, [IRO.Deeds.I.109; III.66]; a gentleman in the parish of St Andrew, Jamaica, probate, 1678, PCC

HIDES, WILLIAM, died in Jamaica, admin., 1656, PCC

HIERN, CHARLES, a physician and surgeon in St Elizabeth parish, Jamaica, a copy will, 1767. [Devon Record Office. 189M]

HIGGIN, ISAAC, from Tooting, Surrey, died in Jamaica on 11 February 1832. [GM.102.383]

HIGGIN, JOHN, born 1816, son of Isaac Higgin, died at Llandovery Estate, Jamaica, on 17 August 1853. [GM.ns40.537]

HIGGIN, THOMAS, born 1830, son of Isaac Higgin in London, died in Jamaica on 9 February 1853. [GM.ns.39.560]

HIGHATT, HENRY, son of Richard Highatt in Bristol, died at Martha Brae, Jamaica, on 23 January 1810. [GM.ns80.384]

HILL, EDWARD, from Jamaica, died in Bristol on 8 February 1815. [GM.85.278]

HILL, FRANCIS, born 1773, from Broxbourne, Hertfordshire, died in Jamaica on 31 January 1850. [GM.ns.33.558]

HILL, RICHARD, a citizen and grocer of London, died in Jamaica, probate, 1680, PCC

HILL, ROGER, a merchant in Port Royal, 1699, 1672. [IRO. Deeds.viii.36; i.89]

HILL, THOMAS, in the parish of St Andrew, Jamaica, probate, 1680, PCC

HILL, WILLIAM, Customs Controller, died in Port Antonio, Jamaica, in April 1793. [GM.63.671]

HINE, ELIZA ANN, daughter of William Hine in Jamaica, married John Rose Cormack MD, from Edinburgh, in London on 4 November 1841. [GM.ns 17.92]

HINGSTON, Mrs SELINA MARIA, born 1830, wife of Captain C. H. Hingston of the 3RD West Indian Regiment, died in Jamaica on 11 April 1854. [GM.ns42.90]

HISME, ANDREW, born 1744, a physician from London, via London aboard the Nancy bound for Jamaica in 1774. [TNA.T47.9/11]

HITCHCOCKE, FRANCIS, a gentleman of Burlescombe, Devon, died in Jamaica, probate, 1657, PCC

THE PEOPLE OF JAMAICA, 1655 TO 1855

HOBART, GEORGE, a Magistrate of St Andrew's and Master in Chancery, died in Jamaica on 19 January 1793. [GM.63.283]

HOBBS, ..., was born in Newcastle, Jamaica, son of T. F. Hobbs, Colonel of the 6th Royal Regiment, on 18 February 1865. [GM.ns2/18/497]

HOBKIRK, Mr, born 1749, a merchant, returning via London aboard the James Daukins for Jamaica in 1774. [TNA.T47.9/11]

HODGES, JOHN, born 1734, died 27 February 1787. Falmouth gravestone, Jamaica]

HODGES, THOMAS, born 1759, a shipwright from Bedford, bound via London aboard the frigate Price for Jamaica in 1775. [TNA.T47.9/11]

HODGSON, ABRAHAM, born 1765, Custos Rotolorum and Assemblyman for St Mary's, died in Jamaica on 11 April 1837. [GM.ns8.102]

HODGSON, I., son of A. Hodgson in Jamaica, married E. Lee Clarke, daughter of G. I. Clarke of Hydehall, in Stockport on 9 August 1831. [GM.ns101.171]

HODGSON, JOSEPH, died 1843. [Falmouth gravestone]; born 1795, from Falmouth, Jamaica, died in Barnes on 25 September 1843. [GM.ns. 20.557]

HOLBROOKE, Captain JOHN, from Bristol, died in Jamaica, probate,1689, PCC

HOLDEN, ROBERT JOHN, from Jamaica, married Elizabeth Holder, daughter of John Holder in Hereford, in Bath on 19 December 1848. [GM.ns31.310]

HOLDEN, ROBERT, in Little Eastcheap, son of Robert Holden from Jamaica, married Anne Kellerman, daughter of Jacob Kellerman from Jamaica, in Worthing, Sussex, on 17 January 1801. [GM.71.93]

THE PEOPLE OF JAMAICA, 1655 TO 1855

HOLDEN, SARAH, born 1750, wife of Robert Holden a sugar baker, died 5 November 1769. [Kingston gravestone, Jamaica]

HOLDER, Mrs, widow of William Holder, and sister of Mrs Pring in Crediton, died in Jamaica on 16 January 1832. [GM.102.383]

HOLDMAN, Mr, a gentleman, to be store-keeper in HM Dockyard in Jamaica, via Portsmouth aboard the Ipswich bound for Jamaica in 1775. [TNA.T47.9/11]

HOLDSWORTH, CHARLES, born 1743, a planter returning to Jamaica from London aboard the St James in 1774. [TNA.T47.9/11]

HOLLAND, JOHN, born 1757, Judge of the Vice Admiralty Court of Jamaica, died 12 January 1804. [St Andrew's gravestone, Jamaica]

HOLLINGWORTH, DAVID, born 1766, settled in Jamaica in 1784, Assemblyman for Manchester and Colonel of Militia, died in Jamaica on 30 July 1840. [GM.ns14.676]

HOLMES, Reverend WILLIAM, son of Robert Holmes in Limerick, in St Anne's, Jamaica, died in Jamaica in 1802. [GM.72.377]

HOME, the Countess of, at Snow Hill, a planter of 1373 acres in St Andrew's parish, Jamaica, in 1754. [TNA.CO137/28/171-196]

HOOD, alias GOLDIER, WILLIAM, a carpenter from Barking, London, late in Jamaica, probate, 1657, PCC

HOOPER, JOHN, fought at the Battle of Sedgemoor in Somerset, on 6 July 1685 against the forces of King James II, captured and transported from Portland Road aboard the Jamaican Merchant of London, master Charles Gardiner, bound for Jamaica in 1685.

HOPKINS, HENRY, a merchant in Port Royal Jamaica, probate, 1677, PCC

HOPKINS, JOSIAS, died in Jamaica, admin, 1656, PCC

THE PEOPLE OF JAMAICA, 1655 TO 1855

HOPPER, THOMAS, born in Ireland, a merchant in Charleston, South Carolina, a Loyalist, moved to Kingston, Jamaica in 1783. [TNA.AO12.51.199-205, etc]

HORLOCK, SAMUEL, born 1740, from Jamaica, died in London in 1825. [GM.95.187]

HORSFORD, ..., son of Lieutenant Colonel Horsford in Jamaica, died in Spanish Town, Jamaica, in 1805. [GM.75.771]

HOUGHTON, RICHARD, a merchant in Port Royal, 1670. [IRO.Deeds.iii.117]

HOUNSBY, JOHN, born 1744, a weaver from Suffolk, bound via Yarmouth aboard the Effingham bound for Jamaica in 1775. [TNA.T47.9/11]

HOUSE, CHRISTIAN, in Colleton County, South Carolina, a Loyalist who moved to Jamaica by 1783. [TNA.AO13.98.311-315]

HOUSE, JAMES, born 1757, a planter from Berwick on Tweed, bound aboard the Jamaica via London for Jamaica in 1774. [TNA.T47.9/11]

HOUSER, HENRY, rector of St Katherine's parish, Jamaica, probate, 1684, PCC

HOW, Mr, a gentleman, emigrated via Portsmouth aboard the Richmond bound for Jamaica in 1775. [TNA.T47.9/11]

HOWARD, CHARLES, Governor of Jamaica, 1709. [ActsPCCol.1708.223]

HOWARD, Sir PHILIP, Governor of Jamaica, 21 January 1685. [CSP.VI.2060]

HOWELL, Mrs ELIZABETH, born 1737, wife of Joseph Howell a shipwright in Jamaica, died 24 July 1779. [Kingston gravestone, Jamaica]

HOWELL, JOHN, a soldier aboard the frigate <u>Torrington</u> at Jamaica, probate, 1656, PCC

HOWELL, THOMAS, fought at the Battle of Sedgemoor in Somerset, on 6 July 1685 against the forces of King James II, captured and transported from Portland Road aboard the <u>Jamaican Merchant of London</u>, master Charles Gardiner, bound for Jamaica in 1685.

HOWTHGATE, Miss, daughter of Joseph Howthgate in Kingston, Jamaica, married Mr Turner an attorney, in London in 1791. [GM.61.582]

HOZIER, JAMES, born 1793, from Jamaica, died in London on 22 November 1846. [GM.ns22.102]

HOZIER, JANE, widow of James Hozier in Jamaica, married James O'Loughlin MD in London on 11 September 1849. [GM.ns32.530]

HUDSON, JOHN, born 1697, Chief Judge, died 7 February 1749. [St Catherine's gravestone, Jamaica]

HUGHES, JOHN, born 1775, a barrister at law, died 1802. [Montego Bay gravestone, Jamaica]

HUGHES, MARY, widow of Thomas Hughes a clerk of Laycock, Wiltshire, late of Walton on Thames, Surrey, died in St Jago de la Vega, Jamaica, probate, 1694, PCC

HUGHES, MATTHEW, born 1700, son of Walter Hughes in Swansea, a shipwright in Kingston, Jamaica, died 1 July 1744, also his son Matthew, born 16 October 1734, died 19 October 1737. [Kingston gravestone, Jamaica]

HUGHES, WALTER, a planter of 1200 acres in St Andrew's parish, Jamaica, in 1754. [TNA.CO137/28/171-196]

HUGHES, Captain WILLIAM, born 1766, of Rose Point Plantation, died in Jamaica on 29 August 1836. [GM.ns6.668]

HULME, J. R., Special Magistrate of Jamaica, papers, 1834-1837. [Staffordshire Record Office, D538.4M]

HUMBERSTONE, Reverend FRANCIS, born 16 July 1791, died 9 August 1819. [Kingston gravestone, Jamaica]

HUME, BENJAMIN, born 1697, died 1773 in Jamaica. [GM.43.470]

HUMMELL, ELIZABETH, born 1756, died 9 November 1821. [Spring Path gravestone, Kingston, Jamaica]

HUMPHREYS, Reverend PHILIP, in Portland, Jamaica, died on 16 January 1834. [GM.104.663]

HUMFREYS, ROBERT, died in Jamaica, admin, 1659, PCC

HUNT, RICHARD, died in Falmouth, Jamaica, in 1803. [GM.73.86]

HUNTER, ROBERT, Governor of Jamaica, letters, 1728-1733. [BM.Newcastle.Add.32758/32778/32781/32782]; died 31 March 1734. [GM.4.330]

HUTTON, ALEXANDER, married Miss Coosens from Lambeth, in Jamaica on 22 August 1775. [GM.45.406]

HYATT, CHARLES, from Jamaica, married Miss Sparks, in London on 24 May1758. [GM.58.244]

HYDE, EDMOND, in Jamaica, died 17 August 1763. [GM.33.565]

IMLAM, JOHN, a poet, died 1845 in Jamaica. [GM.ns25.670]

INGE, ANNE, a widow in St Katherine's, Jamaica, probate, 1697, PCC

INGLE, SPARKES, son of John Ingle in Ashby-de-la-Zouch, died in Kingston, Jamaica, on 29 December 1809. [GM.80.491]

INGLIS, JAMES, from Kingston, Jamaica, died in Walthamstow on 5 November 1814. [GM.84.604]

THE PEOPLE OF JAMAICA, 1655 TO 1855

INGLIS, THOMAS, a merchant in Charleston, South Carolina, a Loyalist soldier, moved to Kingston, Jamaica, by 1784. [TNA.AO12.52.249, etc]

INGLIS, THOMAS, son of Charles Inglis, died in Jamaica on 21 August 1799. [GM.69.1193]

INGRAM, Miss, daughter of Peter Ingram former Provost Marshal of Jamaica, married Frederick Ravencamp of Moore Park, in St George's, Jamaica, in October 1789. [GM.60.83]

INNES, DAVID, a Naval officer, died in Jamaica on 20 August 1807. [GM.77.1075]

INNES, JOHN, a planter of 1273 acres in St Andrew's parish in 1754. [TNA.CO137/28/171-196]

IREDELL, Reverend ARTHUR, of Trinity College, Cambridge, died in Jamaica in November 1804. [GM.75.183]

IREDELL, THOMAS, former President of Jamaica, died there in September 1796. [GM.66.1057]

IRONSIDE, JOHN GILBERT, son of Reverend William Ironside in Houghton-le-Spring, County Durham, died in Springvale, Trelawney, Jamaica, on 14 December 1796. [GM.66.255]

IRVING, JACOB EMILIUS, from Jamaica, married Catherine Humphrey, daughter of Sir J. Humphrey of Boulogne, in Paris on 2 December 1821. [GM.91.641]

IRVING, JACOB EMILIUS, born 1791, from Ironshore, Jamaica, died in Niagara on 7 October 1856. [GM.ns.2/1.780]

IRVING, JACOB EMILIUS, from Jamaica, died in Liverpool in 1816. [GM.86.570]

IRVING, JOHN BEAUFIN, son of J. B. Irving, in Jamaica, married Diana Charlotte Williamson, daughter of Jonathan Williamson in

Lakelands, County Dublin, in Cheltenham on 6 April 1843.
[GM.ns.19.528]

IRVING, W., son of James Irving on Rio Bueno, Jamaica, died on
Iron Shore Wharf, Jamaica, on 22 June 1798. [GM.68.811]

ISRAEL, HENRY, jr., of St Ann's, Jamaica, a petition, 1752.
[ActsPCCol.1745-1766.689]

ISRAEL, JOSEPH, born 1754, a planter, returning to Jamaica via
London aboard the Parnassus in 1774. [TNA.T47.9/11]

ISRAEL, PETER, born 1756, a planter, returning to Jamaica via
London aboard the Parnassus in 1774. [TNA.T47.9/11]

ISRAEL, WILLIAM, born 1757, a planter, returning to Jamaica via
London aboard the Parnassus in 1774. [TNA.T47.9/11]

ISTED, THOMAS, a planter in Jamaica, papers, 1720-1728. [Lincoln
Archives. Ancaster. 9.D.3]

JACKSON, ELIZABETH, daughter of William Jackson, Chief Justice of
Jamaica, married Nathaniel Bogle French jr. of Dulwich, Surrey, on
5 January 1811. [GM.81.85]

JACKSON, EMILY, daughter of S. Jackson of Catherine Hall,
Montego Bay, married Hugo James, in Spanish Town, Jamaica, on
1 July 1817. [GM.87.274]

JACKSON, ISAAC, born 1797, died on Roehampton Estate, St
James, Jamaica, on 3 August 1856. [GM.ns2/1.520]

JACKSON, JANE MARIA, wife of W. H. Jackson, and daughter of
Edward Bullock in Jamaica, died in London on 4 October 1852.
[GM.ns.38.550]

JACKSON, J., widow of J. Jackson the Advocate General of Jamaica,
mother of T. Witter the Attorney General of Jamaica, died 4
September 1811. [GM.81.391]

THE PEOPLE OF JAMAICA, 1655 TO 1855

JACKSON, J., a Special Magistrate, a former Lieutenant of the 94th Regiment, died in Jamaica in 1835. [GM.ns.5.102]

JACKSON, RACHEL, daughter of Samuel Jackson of Catherine Hall, Jamaica, married R. Deans, son of Admiral Deans, in Spanish Town, Jamaica, on 10 April 1820. [GM.90.562]

JACKSON, ROBERT, Captain at Forth Charlotte, Colonel of Militia, Supreme Court Judge, and an Assemblyman, died at Montego Bay, Jamaica, on 26 June 1800. [GM.70.901]

JACKSON, WILLIAM, a mariner in Port Royal, 1680. [IRO.Deeds.13.64]

JACKSON, WILLIAM, born 1732, a former Chief Justice of Jamaica, died inon London on 24 May 1804. [GM.74.487]

JACKSON, ..., son of John Barclay Jackson of the 2nd West Indian Regiment, was born in St Ann's, Jamaica, on 24 December 1864. [GM.ns2/18.232]

JACOBS, LIONEL, son of J. Jacobs a glass manufacturer in Bristol, died in Spanish Town, Jamaica, on 16 November 1812. [GM.83.83]

JACQUET, PHILIP, born 1772, settled in Jamaica in 1787, died there on 26 June 1834. [GM.104.558]

JAMES, CAROLINE HAUGHTON CLARKE, daughter of John H. James in Jamaica, widow of Lieutenant Colonel Clarke of the Grenadier Guards, married Peregrine Taylor Bingley, son of T. B. Bingley of the Bengal Horse Artillery, in Bayswater on 20 October 1852. [GM.ns39.86]

JAMES, CATHERINE HAUGHTON, daughter of J. H. James in Jamaica, married Sir S. Haughton Clarke, in Jamaica on 9 April 1814. [GM.84.514]

JAMES, CHARLES, born 1762, a schoolboy returning home via London aboard the Montague James to Jamaica in 1774, [TNA.T47.9/11]

THE PEOPLE OF JAMAICA, 1655 TO 1855

JAMES, ELIZABETH HAUGHTON, daughter of John Haughton James in Jamaica, died in London on12 December 1850. [GM.ns35.213]

JAMES, ELIZABETH, born 1767, widow of Dr Hugh James in Jamaica, died in Exeter on 13 August 1854. [GM.ns42.410]

JAMES, ELIZABETH, daughter of Thomas James in Enfield, Jamaica, married Reverend Augustus Francis Smith, son of Reverend Rowland Smith of Ilston, Glamorgan, in Littlebourne on 13 May 1863. [GM.ns2/14.785]

JAMES, GEORGE, born 1760, a schoolboy returning home via London aboard the Montague James to Jamaica in 1774, [TNA.T47.9/11]

JAMES, HUGO, in Spanish Town, Jamaica, married Emily Jackson, daughter of S. Jackson of Catherine Hall, Montego Bay, on 1 July 1817. [GM.17.274]

JAMES, JOSEPH, a merchant in Port Royal, Jamaica, probate, 1699, PCC

JAMES, ROBERT, died in Jamaica in 1790. [GM.60.1053]

JAMES, Mrs, wife of William Rhodes James in Spanish Town, died on passage to Jamaica on 7 January 1815. [GM.85.373]

JAMESON, PETER, Secretary to the Governor of Jamaica, died on 30 April 1773. [GM.43.203]

JAMIESON, DAVID, born 1800 in London, died in Jamaica on 6 February 1843. [GM.ns19.556]

JAMIESON, JAMES, an American Loyalist, probably from South Carolina, who was granted land in St Elizabeth parish, Jamaica, in 1782. [TNA]

JAMISON, WILLIAM, from Jamaica, died in Bath in 1797. [GM.67.897]

JARRETT, HERBERT NEWTON, died in Jamaica in 1790.[GM.60.1053]

JARRETT, MARIA, born 1771, widow of Herbert Newton Jarrett in Jamaica, died in Downton, Wiltshire, on 9 December 1831. [GM.101.573]

JARRETT, MARY, daughter of John Jarrett in Jamaica, married John Ashton from Cheshire, in Liverpool in 1790. [GM.60.474]

JEPSON, SYLVESTER, born 1794, died 25 July 1812. [Annotto Bay gravestone, Jamaica]

JERDAN, JOHN STUART, born 1809, son of William Jerdan in Bronton, a Magistrate of Machineal, St Thomas-in-the-East, Jamaica, died on 25 December 1834. [GM.105.334]

JEWELL, WILLIAM, son of John Jewell in Bideford, Devon, died at Montego Bay, Jamaica, on 12 June 1798. [GM.68.223]

JEWER, THOMAS, from Jamaica, died in Bath on 17 April 1798. [GM.68.445]

JOHNSON, CHARLES, a mariner from Stepney, London, died in Port Royal, Jamaica, 1683, PCC

JOHNSON, HEZEKIAH, born 1752, a land surveyor from London, via London aboard the Standlinch bound for Jamaica in 1774. [TNA.T47.9/11]

JOHNSON, JESSY, daughter of John Johnson in St Thomas-in-the-East, Jamaica, married John Walker in London on 8 February 1820. [GM.90.71]

JOHNSON, JOSEPH, born 1760, a cordwainer from London, via London aboard the Nancy bound for Jamaica in 1774. [TNA.T47.9/11]

THE PEOPLE OF JAMAICA, 1655 TO 1855

JOHNSON, Mr, born 1753, a gentleman, to be store-keeper in HM Dockyard in Jamaica, via Portsmouth aboard the Ipswich bound for Jamaica in 1775. [TNA.T47.9/11]

JOHNSTONE, ANDREW, of White Hall, a planter of 308 acres in St Andrew's parish in 1754. [TNA.CO137/28/171-196]

JONES, ELIZABETH, born 1785, widow of Reverend Thomas Arthur Jones in Vere, Jamaica, died in Bromley, Kent, on 6 February 1862. [GM.ns2/12.386]

JONES, Reverend JAMES ALFRED, died in Falmouth, Jamaica, on 8 February 1850. [GM.ns34.99]

JONES, JOHN, from Stepney, London, died in Jamaica, admin., 1656, PCC

JONES, JOHN, fought at the Battle of Sedgemoor in Somerset, on 6 July 1685 against the forces of King James II, captured and transported from Portland Road aboard the Jamaican Merchant of London, master Charles Gardiner, bound for Jamaica in 1685.

JONES, SARAH JOHNSON, daughter of Maurice Jones in Brompton, from Portland, Jamaica, married Henry William Rolle in London on 9 July 1845. [GM.ns24.415]

JOPP, ALEXANDER, in Kingston, Jamaica, died aboard the Ceres on 28 January 1798. [GM.68.444]

JOPP, CHARLES MITCHELL, born 1805, died 8 September 1861. [St Andrew's gravestone, Jamaica]

JORDAN, WILLIAM, born 1739, a gentleman returning to Jamaica via Bristol aboard the Hector in 1775. [TNA.T47.9/11]

JOURDAINE, DANIELL, a merchant in Jamaica, 1672. [IRO.Deeds.V.148]

JUGGINS, THOMAS, from Jamaica, died at Shootershill on 24 March 1807. [GM.77.487]

THE PEOPLE OF JAMAICA, 1655 TO 1855

KAIR, THOMAS, born 1749, a clerk from Ireland, via London aboard the <u>Great Marlow</u> bound for Jamaica in 1774. [TNA.T47.9/11]

KEITH, Sir BASIL, Governor of Jamaica, married Miss Warren in London on 23 July 1773. [GM.43.359]

KELLERMAN, ANNE, daughter of Jacob Kellerman, from Jamaica, married Robert Holden of Little Eastcheap, son of R. Holden from Jamaica, in Watling, Sussex, on 17 January 1801. [GM.71.83]

KELLERMAN, Mrs E., widow of J. Kellerman in Jamaica, married Joseph Bramley of Stamford Hill, in Hackney, London, on 2 May 1801. [GM.71.479]

KELSALL, SARAH, born 1685, died 1734. [St Catherine's gravestone, Jamaica]

KELSAL, SUSAN, daughter of Charles Kelsal in Jamaica, married George Clarke in Westham, Essex, on 12 February 1776. [GM.46.142]

KENRICK, MICHAEL, died in Jamaica, admin., 1656, PCC

KENSILL, HENRY, died in Jamaica, probate, 1657, PCC

KELLERMAN, Miss, daughter of Jacob Kellerman a planter in Jamaica, married Richard Cooke, of Farmhill, in Stroud, Gloucestershire, on 19 June 1793. [GM.63.575]

KELLERMAN, ANNE, daughter of Jacob Kellerman, from Jamaica, married Robert Holden in Little Eastcheap, son of Robert Holden, from Jamaica, in Worthing, Sussex, on 17 January 1801. [GM.71.83]

KELLERMAN, Mrs E., widow of J. Kellerman in Jamaica, married Joseph Bramly of Stanford Hill, in London on 2 May 1801. [GM.71.479]

KELLY, JOHN, died in Jamaica in 1791. [GM.61.187]

THE PEOPLE OF JAMAICA, 1655 TO 1855

KELLY, JOHN, of Tamarind Grove, Househill, died in Jamaica on 18 October 1805. [GM.75.87]

KELLY, JOHN, born 1770, of Green Castle, Jamaica, died 4 November 1813. [GM.83.622]

KELLY, WILLIAM, Captain of the Anotto Bay Company, died in St George's, Jamaica, on 16 November 1789. [GM.60.85]

KELSAL, SUSAN, daughter of Charles Kelsal in Jamaica, married George Clarke in Westham, Essex, on 12 February 1776. [GM.46.142]

KENT, Captain JOHN, of Boston, New England, born 1686, died in Jamaica on 16 September 1732. [Kingston gravestone, Jamaica]

KERR, Dr DAVID, born 1745, a gentleman and a surgeon, emigrated via Portsmouth aboard the Dawes bound for Jamaica in 1775, [TNA.T47.9/11]; in Trelawney, Jamaica, letters, 1783. [NLS.MS3591]

KETTLE, WILLIAM, born 1744, a blacksmith from London, , bound via London aboard the Mars for Jamaica in 1774. [TNA.T47.9/11]

KINCAID, GEORGE, an American Loyalist, probably from South Carolina, who was granted land in St Elizabeth parish, Jamaica, in 1782. [TNA]

KINCAID, Mrs MARION, an American Loyalist, probably from South Carolina, who was granted land in St Elizabeth parish, Jamaica, in 1782. [TNA]

KING, Mrs CHRISTIAN, daughter of Reverend John Campbell of St Andrew's, Jamaica, and wife of William Brooks King, from Jamaica, died in Teignmouth on 5 May 1864. [GM.ns.2/16.812]

KING, FRANCIS, died in Jamaica in 1791. [GM.61.187]

KING, SAMUEL, born 1751, a husbandman from Somerlyton in Suffolk, bound aboard the Norfolk via Yarmouth for Jamaica in 1775. [TNA.T47.9/11]

KING, WILLIAM, in Port Royal, 1662. [IRO. Deeds.x.112]

KING, WILLIAM BROOKS, born 1824, son of James Bryan King in Portland, Jamaica, died in Sydney, New South Wales, on 22 October 1849. [GM.ns33.559]

KIRBY, JOHN, Chief Justice of Jamaica, died in Spanish Town, Jamaica, in 1809. [GM.79.585]

KIRKE, ELIZABETH KING, from Jamaica, married Captain Mayne 'in the Jamaica trade', in London on 30 August 1789. [GM.59.860]

KIRKHAM, Dr, from Leominster, Herefordshire, died in Kingston, Jamaica, on 20 April 1799. [GM.69.717]

KIRKLAND, JAMES, an American Loyalist, probably from South Carolina, who was granted land in St Elizabeth parish, Jamaica, in 1782. [TNA]

KIRKLAND, MOSES, an American Loyalist, probably from South Carolina, who was granted land in St Elizabeth parish, Jamaica, in 1782. [TNA]

KIRTON, LEONARD, from Bermondsey, London, a mariner on the John and Mary, died in Jamaica, probate, 1686, PCC

KNIGHT, LEWIS, from Jamaica, died in London on 10 March 1813. [GM.83.389]

KNIGHT, SAMUEL, born 1685, son of Dr Samuel Knight, died 7 March 1709. [St Catherine's gravestone, Jamaica]

KNIGHT, SUSANNAH, born 1742, died 20 January 1794. [Shaw Park, St Ann's, gravestone, Jamaica]

KNITT, WILLIAM HENRY, son of Reverend William Smith Knitt of Bawdrip, Somerset, died in Jamaica o 10 September 1851. [GM.n36.666]

KNOWLES, CHARLES, Governor of Jamaica, papers 1750s. [Sussex Archaeological Society, Fuller mss]

KNOWLES, Sir CHARLES HENRY, born 24 August 1754 in Jamaica, son of Admiral Sir Charles Knowles the Governor there, died 28 November 1831. [GM.101.564]

KNOX, GEORGE, an American Loyalist, probably from South Carolina, who was granted land in St Elizabeth parish in 1782. [TNA]

KNOX, THOMAS, an American Loyalist, probably from South Carolina, who was granted land in St Elizabeth parish in 1782. [TNA]

KNOX, WILLIAM, an American Loyalist, probably from South Carolina, who was granted land in St Elizabeth parish in 1782. [TNA]

LABERT, SAMUEL, born 1713, died 1786. Montego Bay gravestone, Jamaica]

LAGUNA, DANIEL LOPEZ, born 1635 in Portugal, moved to France, educated in Spain, imprisoned by the Inquisition. Escaped and emigrated to Jamaica, poet and author of *Espejo fiel de Vidas*, died in Jamaica in 1730.

LAING, Reverend DAVID, of St Peter College, Cambridge, son of David Laing in Jamaica, married Mary Elizabeth West, daughter of John West, in Jamaica on 14 April 1824. [GM.94.369]

LAKE, RICHARD, jr., died in Jamaica IN 1801. [GM.71.770]

LAMB, JOHN, a mariner, died aboard the <u>Swan</u> at Jamaica, probate, 1692, PCC

LAMB, THOMAS, a merchant from Jamaica, in London, probate, 1693, PCC

THE PEOPLE OF JAMAICA, 1655 TO 1855

LAMBDEN, NATHANIEL, born 1753, a bricklayer from Berkshire, bound via London aboard the Henry for Jamaica in 1774. [TNA.T47.9/11]

LAMBERT, Major General, born 1786, died 4 January 1848. [St Andrew's gravestone, Jamaica]

LAMBIE, WILLIAM, from Jamaica, married Elizabeth Dundas Crichton daughter of Patrick Crichton in Jamaica, in Edinburgh in 1820. [GM.90.563]

LAMERA, AARON, executor of Jacob de Castro, a petitioner in Jamaica, 1752. [ActsPCCol.1745-1766, 151]

LA MOTTE, LEWIS, a barrister, died in Spanish Town, Jamaica, on 23 August 1814. [GM.84.498]

LA MOTTE, LEWIS JOHN, son of Lewis La Motte in Jamaica, died in Bremen on 11 October 1848. [GM.ns30.671]

LA MOUSIER, BELDAM, born 1788 in Cailles, St Louis, died in Kingston on 10 Juin 1838. [Spring Path gravestone, Kingston, Jamaica]

LAMPKIN, SYMONDS, in Jamaica, died in April 1753. [GM.23.248]

LAND, THOMAS, a solicitor, son of Reverend Thomas Land in Tiverton, died in Spanish Town, Jamaica, in October 1850. [GM.ns35.110]

LANDER, GEORGE, died in Jamaica, admin., 1658, PCC

LANE, CHRISTIAN, born 1785, wife of James Seton of St Thomas in the Vale, died 28 September 1808. [St Catherine's gravestone, Jamaica]

LANE, RICHARD, a barber from Trinity, Minories, London, died in Port Royal, probate, 1692, PCC

LANG, MALCOLM, a planter of 150 acres in St Andrew's parish in 1754. [TNA.CO137/28/171-196]

THE PEOPLE OF JAMAICA, 1655 TO 1855

LANGDON, MICAH, son of Mrs Langdon in Bristol, died on passage from Jamaica on 4 July 1806. [GM.76.874]

LANGFORD, ABRAHAM, in Thames Street, Port Royal, in 1659. [BM.Add.ms 12423.101]

LANGLEY, THOMAS, MD, died in Jamaica in 1791. [GM.61.187]

LATIMER, RICHARD, from Kingston, Jamaica, died in Crumlin, Ireland, on 30 October 1813. [GM.83.622]

LA TOUCHE, MARY, born 1757, widow of John Digges La Touche in Jamaica, died in Tunbridge Wells in 1842. [GM.ns19.107]

LA TROBE, FREDERIC BENJAMIN, born 1804, son of Reverend C. J. La Trobe, died in Jamaica on 11 December 1841. [GM.ns.18.223]

LAWES, Sir NICHOLAS, Governor of Jamaica, 25 July 1717.

LAWRENCE, JAMES, born 1739, a gentleman from London, bound via London aboard the Henry for Jamaica in 1774. [TNA.T47.9/11]

LAWRENCE, JAMES CHARLES, of Hazlenymph and St Ives, died in Hazelnymph, Jamaica, in 1813. [GM.81.679]

LAWRENCE, JOHN, born 1672, died 7 January 1718. [St Catherine's gravestone, Jamaica]

LAWRENCE, Reverend RICHARD BRISSETT, born 1790, died 13 October 1821. [St Catherine's gravestone, Jamaica]

LAWRENCE, THOMAS, from Kingston, Jamaica, late in Cheapside, died on 29 January 1805. [GM.75.881]

LAWRIE, Mrs, sister of Dr Steele in Jamaica, died in Kentish Town on 7 August 1798. [GM.68.729]

LAWS, JAMES, died in Jamaica on 16 April 1732. [GM.4.330]

LAWS, Sir NICHOLAS, Governor of Jamaica, died there in 1731. [GM.1.355]

THE PEOPLE OF JAMAICA, 1655 TO 1855

LAWTON, CHARLES HENRY, son of Reverend J. Thomas Lawton in Elmswell, Suffolk, died in Hampton, Jamaica, on 5 March 1846. [GM.ns25.670]

LAWTON, FREDERICK, son of Reverend J. T. Lawton in Elmswell, Suffolk, died in Jamaica on 13 May 1852. [GM.ns38.211]

LAYTON, THOMAS, born 1742, a horse jockey from Malton, , via Hull aboard the Jamaica Packet bound for Jamaica in 1774. [TNA.T47.9/11]

LEAN, WILLIAM, from Veryon, Cornwall, a mariner aboard the Diamond, died in Jamaica, probate, 1693, PCC

LEAMY, EDMUND, born 1829, died 14 November 1855. [Annotto Bay gravestone, Jamaica]

LEE, EDWARD, died in Jamaica, admin., 1657, PCC

LEE, GEORGE, from Jamaica, died on 4 October 1757. [GM.27.482]

LEE, JAMES, born 1753, a physician and Member of the Privy Council of Jamaica, died 30 May 1821 in the Gulf of Florida on passage to England. [St Catherine's gravestone, Jamaica]

LEECH, WILLIAM, vendue master in Jamaica, letters, 1750-1753. [BM. Newcastle. Add.32731]32733/33066]

LEGARD, RICHARD, son of Sir Digby Legard, died in Jamaica on 6 June 1818. [GM.88.373]

LEGER, ADELAIDE, born 1752 in Leogane, St Dominique, died 26 August 1828. . [Spring Path, Kingston, gravestone, Jamaica]

LEIGH, Captain, a planter in Jamaica, died on 31 October 1742, [SM.12.502]

LEIGH, ELIZABETH BURKE, daughter of Thomas Leigh, died in Liguana, Jamaica, in November 1801. [GM.72.181]

LEISON, JOHN, died in Jamaica, admin.1657, PCC

THE PEOPLE OF JAMAICA, 1655 TO 1855

LEITCH, COLIN, died in Jamaica in 1791. [GM.61.186]

LEMING, THOMAS, born 1746, a gardener from Yorkshire, bound via London aboard the Britannia for Jamaica in 1773. [TNA.T47.9/11]

LEONI, Mr, 'the celebrated singer', died in Jamaica in October 1796. [GM.67.252]

LE PENE, ..., master of the Bonaventure [formerly the New Garden of Flushing] a privateer at Port Royal in 1659. [BM.Add.mss.12423]

LESLIE, GEORGE, born 1760, son of James Leslie, a former Captain of the 15th Regiment, died in Spring Gardens, St Thomas-in-the-East, Jamaica, on 18 December 1800. [GM.71.185]

LESTER, FRANCIS, a merchant in Jamaica in 1672. [IRO.I.114]

LEVI, MICHAEL, born 1765, from Kingston, Jamaica, died in London on 12 April 1845. [GM.ns23.671]

LEVI, MOSES, born 1749, a poulterer from Paddington, with Hannah his wife, born 1756, via London aboard the Princess Carolina bound for Jamaica in 1774. [TNA.T47.9/11]

LEVY, Captain MATTHEW, born 1770, a trader at Annotto Bay, died 8 July 1823, also his son Matthew Levy, born 1799, died on 8 October 1820 on Quebec Estate. [Annotto Bay gravestone, Jamaica]

LEVYS, HENRIETTA, born 1772, widow of Philip Levys in Jamaica, died in Notting Hill on 11 September 1852. [GM.ns38.439]

LEWIN, JAMES, a merchant, born 1718, died September 1751. [Kingston gravestone, Jamaica]

LEWIS, EDWIN, died in Jamaica in 1791. [GM.61,652]

LEWIS, H.L., a merchant, died in Kingston, Jamaica, on 18 March 1816. [GM.86.474]

LEWIS, JAMES, born 1778, former Speaker if the Jamaica Assembly and Advocate General, died in London on 18 August 1847. [GM.ns28.440]

LEWIS, JOHN, a printer, died in Jamaica in 1791. [GM.61,1065]

LEWIS, JOHN, in Jamaica, letters, 1795-1796. [BM.Windham.Add.37914]

LEWIS, JOHN, born 1749, Assemblyman for Westmoreland, Chief Justice of Jamaica, died 17 September 1820. [Harmony Hall gravestone, Westmoreland, Jamaica]

LEWIS, MARY, born 1758, with from London, with Maria Lewis born 1761, and Catharine Lewis born 1763, emigrating via Portsmouth aboard the Judith and Hilaria bound for Jamaica in 1776. [TNA.T47.9/11]

LEWIS, MATTHEW GREGORY, born 1773, an author, died on passage from Jamaica to England in July 1818.[GM.88.183]

LEWIS, REBECCA, probate, Jamaica, 1735. [BM.MS.21,931]

LEWIS, SAMUEL, a merchant in Jamaica, 1669. [IRO.Deeds.iii.21]

LEWIS, SARAH, daughter of William Lewis in Jamaica, married Robert Sewell, in 1775. [GM.45.606]

LEWIS, WILLIAM, born 1747, an attorney at law from London, bound via London aboard the West Indian for Jamaica in 1774. [TNA.T47.9/11]

LEWIS, WILLIAM FREDERICK, born 1814, son of James Lewis, Commissioner for Slave Compensation, and Supreme Court Judge of Jamaica, died in London on 11 December 1856. [GM.ns2/2.123]

LEYBOURNE, S., son of Governor Leybourne, died aboard the Duke in Jamaica in 1782. [GM.52.454]

LIGHTERMAN, HENRY, a gentleman from Southwark, London, died in Jamaica, probate, 1700, PCC

LIGHTFOOT, SAMUEL, born 1749, a surgeon from London, bound via London aboard the Henry for Jamaica in 1774. [TNA.T47.9/11]

LIMBERY, ANDREW, a mariner from Bristol, died in Jamaica, probate, 1689, PCC

LINDO, ESTHER, daughter of Alexander Lindo, married A. M. Bellisario in Jamaica in 1791. [GM.61.774]

LINDSAY, Reverend JOHN, of St Catherine's, Jamaica, died in Spanish Town, Jamaica, on 3 November 1788. [GM.59.178]

LINGING, JOHN, born 1788 in Kennington, died in St Anne's, Jamaica, in 1810. [GM.80.192]

LINWOOD, S. WHALLEY, son of Mrs Linwood in Leicester, died in Jamaica in 1801. [GM.71.170]

LIPSCOMBE, CHRISTOPHER, Bishop of Jamaica, married Miss Pope, daughter of E. Pope , in London on 27 July 1824. [GM.94.176]

LIPSCOMBE, CHRISTOPHER, Bishop of Jamaica, born 1782, son of Reverend William Lipscombe in Walbury, Northallerton, died in St Thomas on 4 April1843. [GM.ns20.201]

LIPSCOMBE, FRANCES EVES, wife of Dr Lipscombe the Bishop of Jamaica, died at Perkins Pen, Jamaica, on 27 April 1825. [GM.95.652]

LITTILL, Lieutenant Robert, aboard the Jersey at Jamaica, a letter, 1711. [HMC.23]

LITTLE, AARON, died in Jamaica in 1791. [GM.61.186]

LLOYD, ARTHUR, and his wife Alice, in Queen Street, Port Royal, 1670s. [Jamaica Archives, inventory, liber i]

LOADER, JACOB, a mariner from Deptford, died in Port Royal, Jamaica, 1692, PCC

LOCKYER, THOMAS and ALICE, drapers in Honey Lane, Port Royal, before 1692. [IRO.Deeds.i.154]

LOGONA, LOPER DAVID, probate Jamaica 1735. [BM. Add.ms21,931]

LOGONA, LOPER CLARON, probate Jamaica 1743. [BM.Add.ms21,931]

LOMAS, WILLIAM, born 1741, a cordwainer from Northampton, , via London aboard the Nancy bound for Jamaica in 1774. [TNA.T47.9/11]

LOMEGO, AARON, in Jamaica, probate, 1747, PCC

LOMEGO, AARON, in Jamaica, probate, 1807, PCC

LOMEGO, ESTER, in Jamaica, probate, 1767, PCC

LONDON, RALPH, died in Jamaica, admin.1657, PCC

LONDON, WILLIAM, a gentleman from London, died in Jamaica, probate, 1685, PCC

LONG, EDWARD, a planter in Lucky Valley, Claredon parish, Jamaica, 1777, [Suffolk Record Office, HA18.GD1]

LONG, SAMUEL, an Assemblyman, died in Jamaica in 1757. [GM.27.189]

LONG, SOPHIA LOUISA HENRIETTA, born 1803, daughter of Edward Long in Jamaica, and wife of Colonel Lloyd Watkins in Pennoyre, died inBath on 27 May 1851. [GM.ns36.102]

LONGWORTH, JOHN, incumbent of the church in Port Royal, 1679. [IRO.Deeds.13.64]

LOPEZ, ABRAHAM RODRIGUEZ, a Jewish merchant, died in St Jago-de-la-Vega, Jamaica, 13 March1768. [GM.58.933]

THE PEOPLE OF JAMAICA, 1655 TO 1855

LOPEZ, CATHERINE, born 1672, died in Kingston, Jamaica, on 28 August 1806. [GM.75.1075]

LOPES, MORDECAI R., in Jamaica, probate, 1796, PCC.

LOPES, MOSES PARRO, probate, Jamaica, 1733. [BM.Add.ms.21,931]

LOPEZ, RODRINGES ABRAHAM, probate, Jamaica, 1741. [BM.Add.ms 21,931]

LOPEZ, RODRINGES M., probate, Jamaica, 1743. [BM.Add.ms.21,931]

LORD, WILLIAM, master of the 20 ton Sarah trading from Port Royal, 1680s. [TNA.CO145.13.17/30/50/61/229]

LOUSADA, AARON BARUH, a petitioner in Jamaica, 1752. [ActsPCCol.1745-1766.151]

LOUZADA, ARON, in Jamaica, 1768, PCC.

LOUSADA, DANIEL BARUH, in Jamaica, probate, 1769, PCC

LOUSADA, EMANUEL BARUH, a merchant from Jamaica, then in Stoke Newington, probate, 1807. PCC

LOUSADA, JACOB BARUH, in Jamaica, probate, 1752, PCC

LOUSADA, RACHEL BARUH, a widow in Jamaica, probate, 1807, PCC

LOWE, PENELOPE, from Jamaica, married Roger Tuckfield in Devon on 22 February 1755. [GM.25.138]

LOWREY, Captain JOSEPH, from Jamaica, died in Bristol on 21 December 1806. [GM.75.185]

LUCAS, SAMPSON, from Kingston, Jamaica, died in London on 14 April 1813. [GM.83.492]

THE PEOPLE OF JAMAICA, 1655 TO 1855

LUNAN, JOHN, in Spanish Town, Jamaica, letter, 1819. [University of London.AL.253]

LUNDIE, Mrs MARY ANN, wife of Thomas Lundie, from Jamaica, died in Liverpool on 16 March 1844. [GM.ns21.555]

LYNCH, JOHN, born 1737, a farmer from Ireland, bound via London aboard the Nancy bound for Jamaica in 1774. [TNA.T47.9/11]

LYNCH, P., died in Jamaica on 30 September 1817. [GM.87.561]

LYNCH, Sir THOMAS, from Esher, Kent, died in Jamaica on 24 August 1684, probate, 1691, PCC; Jamaica Archives, inventories.i]; Governor of Jamaica, 28 July 1681. [CSP.VI.194]

LYON, BENJAMIN, in Jamaica, probate, 1780, PCC

LYON, BENJAMIN,SON OF Benjamin Lyon in Jamaica, died in Spanish Town, Jamaica, on 5 September 1800. [GM.70.1107]

LYON, ANNE, daughter of Benjamin Lyon in Jamaica, married J. Kerr Jordan, son of Captain J. Dudley Jordan, and grandson of Jacob Jordan in Lower Canada, in Clifton on 10 August 1845. [GM.ns24.520]

LYON, GEORGE, a barrister, died in Spanish Town, Jamaica, in January 1799. [GM.69.347]

LYON, JOHN, an American Loyalist, probably from South Carolina, who was granted land in St Elizabeth parish, Jamaica, in 1782. [TNA]

LYTTELTON, Sir CHARLES, Deputy Governor of Jamaica, an account roll, 1661-1663, [Birmingham City Library, 351959]

LYTTELTON, WILLIAM HENRY, was appointed Captain General and Governor-in-Chief of Jamaica on 3 June 1760. [Birmingham City Library, 399926]; Governor of Jamaica, brother of Lord Lyttelton, married Miss Macartney on 2 June 1761. [GM.21.284]; a son was born on 26 October 1763. [GM.34.146]

MCANUFF, JOHN CLINTON, Master of Chancery in Jamaica, and Judge of the Supreme Court of Jamaica, died on Hopewell Estate, Jamaica, in 1819. [GM.88.655]

MCCARTHY, ALEXANDER, a military officer, died 1820. [Falmouth gravestone, Jamaica]

MCCLALAND SARAH, in Nottingham, daughter of Joseph McClaland in Kingston, Jamaica, married John Mayne of Houndsgate, Nottingham, in Dublin on 16 June 1798. [GM.68.624]

MCCLELLAND, ROBERT, died 15 September 1860. [Kingston gravestone, Jamaica]

MCCOMBE, HUGH, an American Loyalist, probably from South Carolina, who was granted land in St Elizabeth parish, Jamaica, in 1782. [TNA]

MCCORNOCK, THOMAS, Custos of St Thomas in the East, Jamaica, died in December 1848. [GM.ns31.335]

MCCROUGH, ..., a planter of 1000 acres in St Andrew's parish, Jamaica, in 1754. [TNA.CO137/28/171-196]

MCDONALD, ALEXANDER, an American Loyalist, probably from South Carolina, who was granted land in St Elizabeth parish, Jamaica, in 1782. [TNA]

MCDONALD, ANGUS, an American Loyalist, probably from South Carolina, who was granted land in St Elizabeth parish, Jamaica, in 1782. [TNA]

MCDONALD, PETER, a planter from Charleston, South Carolina, a Loyalist, who was granted land in St Elizabeth parish, Jamaica, in 1782. [TNA.A13.91.210-214]

THE PEOPLE OF JAMAICA, 1655 TO 1855

MCGEACHY, EDWARD, Crown Surveyor of Jamaica, letters, 1846. [BM.Add.40586.f196; 40593.f140]

MCGILCHRIST, DANIEL, born 1721, a gentleman returning to Jamaica via Bristol aboard the Hector in 1775. [TNA.T47.9/11]

MCGILLIVRAY, JOHN, an American Loyalist, probably from South Carolina, who was granted land in St Elizabeth parish, Jamaica, in 1782. [TNA]

MCGILLIVRAY, LACHLAN, an American Loyalist, probably from South Carolina, who was granted land in St Elizabeth parish, Jamaica, in 1782. [TNA]

MCGILLIVRAY, LACHLAN, jr., an American Loyalist, probably from South Carolina, who was granted land in St Elizabeth parish, Jamaica, in 1782. [TNA]

MCGRATH, SARA, daughter of George McGrath in Charlemont, Jamaica, married Captain Dawson R. Evans of the 6th Royal Regiment, in St Thomas in the Vale, Jamaica, on 4 May 1865. [GM.ns2/19.106]

MCKAY, FRANCIS, an American Loyalist, probably from South Carolina, who was granted land in St Elizabeth parish, Jamaica, in 1782. [TNA]

MACKAY, GEORGE, a planter of 11 acres in St Andrew's parish, Jamaica, in 1754. [TNA.CO137/28/171-196]

MCKAY, JOHN, an American Loyalist, probably from South Carolina, who was granted land in St Elizabeth parish, Jamaica, in 1782. [TNA]

MACKAY, RUPERT, in Jamaica, a bond, 4 June 1785. [NRS.RD2.238/2.894]

THE PEOPLE OF JAMAICA, 1655 TO 1855

MCKAY, SAMUEL, an American Loyalist, probably from South Carolina, who was granted land in St Elizabeth parish, Jamaica, in 1782. [TNA]

MCKAY, STEPHEN, an American Loyalist, probably from South Carolina, who was granted land in St Elizabeth parish, Jamaica, in 1782. [TNA]

MCKENZIE, GEORGE, born 1757, a book-keeper from London, bound via London aboard the Capel for Jamaica in 1774. [TNA.T47.9/11]

MCKENZIE, JOHN, an American Loyalist, probably from South Carolina, who was granted land in St Elizabeth parish, Jamaica, in 1782. [TNA]

MACKENZIE, MARY, late of Claredon parish, Jamaica, now of Exeter, Devon, married Philip Cornish of Saltash, Cornwall, 1775. [Shropshire Record Office, 549/77]

MCKENZIE, PETER, born 1754, a planter returning to Jamaica aboard the Susanna in 1774. [TNA.T47.9/11]

MCKINNON, Mrs HELEN, an American Loyalist, probably from South Carolina, who was granted land in St Elizabeth parish, Jamaica, in 1782. [TNA]

MCKINNON, SAMUEL, an American Loyalist, probably from South Carolina, who was granted land in St Elizabeth parish, Jamaica, in 1782. [TNA]

MCMILLAN, WILLIAM, son of Robert McMillan in Liverpool, died in Jamaica on 6 October 1800. [GM.71.185]

MCMURDO, WILLIAM MUIR, born 1758, a merchant in Kingston, died 25 July 1795. . [Kingston gravestone, Jamaica]

MCNAMARA, JOHN, a merchant in Jamaica, died aboard the Snow River on his passage from Jamaica on 2 August 1815. [GM.85.376]

MCNEAL, Miss, daughter of Thomas McNeal, Custos of Westmoreland, Jamaica, married Captain Henry Turner master of the West India on 25 January 1842. [GM.ns17.429]

MCNEIL, DANIEL, an American Loyalist, probably from South Carolina, who was granted land in St Elizabeth parish, Jamaica, in 1782. [TNA]

MCNEIL, MARGARET, an American Loyalist, probably from South Carolina, who was granted land in St Elizabeth parish in Yarmouth, Jamaica, in 1782. [TNA]

MCNEIL, PETER, an American Loyalist, probably from South Carolina, who was granted land in St Elizabeth parish, Jamaica in 1782. [TNA]

MCPHERSON, DONALD, an American Loyalist, probably from South Carolina, who was granted land in St Elizabeth parish, Jamaica, in 1782. [TNA]

MCQUEEN, DANIEL, a planter of 800 acres in St Andrew's parish in 1754. [TNA.CO137/28/171-196]

MACRAGH, DENIS, a gentleman, and his wife Margery, in High Street, Port Royal, Jamaica, 1673. [IRO.Deeds.xi.104]

MABELLE, MARGARET, daughter of F. Mabelle in Jamaica, married W. Farquharson, Lieutenant in the Royal Artillert, in Ealing on 22 July 1823. [GM.93.272]

MAINETT, JACOB, a merchant in Port Royal, Jamaica, probate, 1679, PCC

MAINETT, JAMES, in Port Royal, Jamaica, will, 1687, PCC

MAIS, FRANCES DUN, daughter of S. W. Mais, Custos of Port Royal, Jamaica, married Reverend William Edward Pierce in St David's, Jamaica, on 5 July 1854. [GM.ns2/17.377]

MAIS, HENRY P., of Messrs John and Henry Mais in Kingston, Jamaica, died there on 3 November 1825. [GM.96.95]

MAIS, JOHN, born 1775, died in Spanish Town, Jamaica, on 9 October 1853. [GM.ns41.439]

MAIS, Reverend JOHN LESLIE, of Spanish Town, Jamaica, married Julie Caroline Hill, daughter of Captain Henry Hill of the 57th Regiment, in St Andrew's, Jamaica, on 29 January 1856. [GM.ns.45.612]

MAIS, MARTHA, wife of John Mais in Kingston, Jamaica, died in London on 15 April 1841. [GM.ns15.554]

MAN, FRANCIS, bound for Jamaica in 1668, [IRO.Deeds.I.72]; a merchant in Jamaica in 1674, [IRO.Deeds.i.214]; probate, 1676, PCC

MANN, Reverend ISAAC, of Caius College, Cambridge, 1800, died in Kingston, Jamaica, in 1829. [GM.99.377]; born 1777, late Rector of Kingston and chaplain to the Provincial Grand Lodge and past Master of the Sussex Lodge, number8, died 1 November 1828. [Kingston gravestone, Jamaica]

MAN, Major JOHN, son of Francis Man, a merchant and planter in Jamaica, dead by 1668. [IRO.Deeds.I.72]

MANN, MARY, widow of Reverend Isaac Mann in Kingston, Jamaica, died in Lee on 30 August 1850. [GM.ns34.452]

MANN, Mr, died at Montego Bay, Jamaica, in 1800. [GM.70.905]

MANBY, AARON, a saddler in Kingston, Jamaica, probate, 1780, PCC

MANNERS, ROGER, died in Jamaica, admin, 1657, PCC

MANNING, THOMAS, born 1744, an ostler from Yarmouth, bound via Yarmouth aboard the Effingham bound for Jamaica in 1775. [TNA.T47.9/11]

THE PEOPLE OF JAMAICA, 1655 TO 1855

MARCELL, HENRIETTA, born 1820, died 1 February 1842. . [Spring Path, Kingston, gravestone, Jamaica]

MARCH, C., died in Jamaica n 1790. [GM.60.766]

MARCH, MARY, born 1801,wife of Thomas March, died 6 November 1820. [Kingston gravestone, Jamaica]

MARKLAND, JOHN EDWARD, born 1792, from Jamaica, died in Caen, Normandy, on 5 July 1863. [GM.ns2/15.248]

MARLER, FRANCIS, from London, died in Jamaica, admin., 1659, PCC

MARSDEN, RICHARD, born 1764, a merchant, died 15 October 1808. [Kingston gravestone, Jamaica]

MARSH, EMMELINE ADRIANA, born 1792, wife of John Milbourne Marsh the Deputy Postmaster General, died in Kingston, Jamaica, on 15 September 1812. [GM.82.670]

MARSH, FRANCES LUCY, daughter of Milbourne Marsh, and niece of Sir Francis Forbes the Chief Justice of New South Wales, married George Foster Wise, son of Edward Wise of Bembridge, Isle of Wight, in Scone, New South Wales, on 21 June 1842. [GM.ns19.197]

MARSH, JOHN MILBOURNE AUGUSTUS, son of J. M. Marsh the Postmaster General of Jamaica, married Grace Elizabeth Pinnock, daughter of Philip Pinnock in Jamaica, in London on 26 January 1848. [GM.ns29.422]

MARSH, WILLIAM, born 1791, son of Cornelius March in Toxford, died in Kingston, Jamaica, on 25 April 1820. [GM.90.186]

MARSHALL, ANNA, daughter of Reverend Edward Marshall in Jamaica, married J. Binney, a Lieutenant of the Royal Navy, son of H. N. Binney in Nova Scotia, in Putney, London, 1822. [GM.92.640]

THE PEOPLE OF JAMAICA, 1655 TO 1855

MARSTON, CHARITY JANE, widow of J. Marston in Jamaica, died in London on 22 January 1832. [GM.102.185]

MARSTON, NATHANIEL, from Jamaica, died in London on 18 October 1826. [GM.26.473]

MARTIN, EDWARD, in Jamaica, letters, around 1750. [Kent Archives, U23C14]

MARTIN, JAMES, died in Jamaica, admin., 1658, PCC

MARTIN, JESSY, born 1801, daughter of George Marshall in Spanish Town, Jamaica, died on 29 June 1819. [GM.89.90]

MARTIN, LEWIS BURWELL, born 1737, brother of Samuel Martin in Whitehaven, Representative for St Elizabeth's, and a judge in Jamaica, die in October 1782. [GM.53.181]

MARTIN, RICHARD, formerly in Charleston, settled in Jamaica by 1783, affidavit in favour of Thomas Hopper. [TNA.AO109.162]

MARTIN, WILLIAM, master of the ship Port Royal of Bristol, died in Jamaica, probate, 1692, PCC

MARTIN, ..., daughter of Albin Martin in Stilton, Dorset, was born in Naples, Jamaica, on 2 November 1842. [GM.ns18.650]

MARTINES, LUIS, born 1808 in Carthagena, died 30 September 1826. [Spring Path gravestone, Kingston, Jamaica]

MASKALL, HENRY, formerly in Charleston, settled in Jamaica by 1783, affidavit in favour of Thomas Hopper. [TNA.AO101.211]

MASON, Dr DAVID, a Councillor of Jamaica, died in Savanna-la-Mar on 6 April 1862. [GM.ns2/13.112]

MASON, Dr ROBERT, in St Mary's, Jamaica, died in October 1792. [GM.62.1220]

MASSIAS, SAMUEL, probate, 1747, Jamaica. [BM.Add.ms 21,931]

MASSIE, JANE, daughter of George Massie in Jamaica, died in Kew on 16 December 1795. [GM.65.1059]

MASTERS, ELIZABETH, born 1708, died 14 May 1737. [Kingston gravestone, Jamaica]

MATTHEWS, E. K., Captain of the 5th West Indian Regiment, son of Etherington Thomas Matthews in St Catherine's, Jamaica, died in St Lucia on 15 January 1810. [GM.80.491]

MATTHEWS, PETER, born 1765, died 24 December 1818. . [Spring Path, Kingston, gravestone, Jamaica]

MATTHEWS, ROBERT, in Jamaica, deceased, papers, 1728-1751. [Glamorgan Record Office. D/DF.F21-25]

MATTHEWS, Captain THOMAS, a merchant of High Street, Port Royal, deceased before 22 April 1676, inventory. [IRO]

MATHISON, GILBERT, Judge of the Grand Court St Jago-de-la-Vega, Trelawney, Jamaica, died in 1774. [GM.44.390]

MAULIN, Mr, died in Kingston, Jamaica, in 1793. [GM.63.1152]

MAXWELL, WILLIAM, born 1760, an attorney at law, died 20 May 1802. [Kingston gravestone, Jamaica]

MAY, Reverend CHARLES T., died in Strathnavar, Buff Bay, Jamaica, on 29 September 1866. [GM.ns3/2.837]

MAY, JAMES, WESTERMAN, of Messrs O'Reilly, Hill, May and Company, in Jamaica, died in London on 8 June 1814.]GM.84.699]

MAY, ROSE HERRINS, a Councillor in Jamaica, died in Spanish Town in 1791. [GM.91.971]

MAYAN, VICTORIN, born1794, died 17 May 1816. [Spring Path gravestone, Kingston, Jamaica]

MAYHEW, ALICE MARIA ELIZABETH, daughter of Reverend William Mayhew in St Andrew's, Jamaica, married George Lee Chandler, a

Captain of the Royal Artillery, at Halfwaytree Church, Jamaica, on 4 December 1862. [GM.ns299/14.369]

MAYLIN, ISAACK, a gentleman from Stepney, London, died in Jamaica, probate, 1691, PCC

MEANY, BRYAN, a surgeon from Waterford, died in Jamaica, 1795. [GM.65.616]

MEECH, WILLIAM, son of Mr Meech a surgeon apothecary in Sherbourne, Dorset, died in Jamaica in August 1800. [GM.70.1290]

MELHADO, JUDITH, born 1788, widow of Daniel Melhado, from Jamaica, died in London on 9 February 1853. [GM.ns39.335]

MELLOR, ABNER, born 1731, died 11 September 1801, his wife, Mary, born 1734, died 27 June 1796, son William Mellor, born 1761, died 16 July 1790, and daughter Dorothy, born 1772, died 7 November 1778. [Kingston gravestone, Jamaica]

MELMOTH, JOHN, brother of J. P. Melmoth, died in Jamaica in 1845. [GM.ns25.446]

MENDES, ABRAHAM DE SOZA, an alien in Jamaica, was granted denization on 9 September 1670. [Patent Office, 22 Car ii]

MEERES, PAYTON, died in Jamaica, admin., PCC

MEMELL, CHARLES, born 1783, died 23 September 1823. [Annotto Bay gravestone, Jamaica]

MENZIES, ALEXANDER, a planter of 81 acres in St Andrew's parish in 1754. [TNA.CO137/28/171-196]

MENZIES, EDWARD, born 1787, from Kingston, Jamaica, died in New Scone, Perthshire, on 12 August 1852. [GM.ns38.434]

MEREDITH, JOHN, a merchant in London, died in Jamaica, probate, 1684, PCC

THE PEOPLE OF JAMAICA, 1655 TO 1855

MEREDITH, WILLIAM, born 1728, from Montgomeryshire, died 13 July 1770. [Kingston gravestone, Jamaica]

MERRIFIELD, WILLIAM, died in St Anne's, Jamaica, in November 1801. [GM.72.1801]

METCALFE, Sir CHARLES, Governor of Jamaica, papers, 1840-1842. [Lincolnshire Archives. Monson. 30.vi]

METYARD, JOHN, fought at the Battle of Sedgemoor in Somerset, on 6 July 1685 against the forces of King James II, captured and transported from Portland Road aboard the Jamaican Merchant of London, master Charles Gardiner, bound for Jamaica in 1685.

MEYERS, HENRY, born 1804, son of T. P. Meyers in Battle, Sussex, and Jamaica, died in Kent on 24 February 1820. [GM.90.283]

MEYLER, Mrs, wife of Jeremiah Meyler, from Jamaica, died in Bath on 26 December 1788. [GM.58.1183]

MICHELL, WILLIAM, Judge of the Vice Admiralty Court of Jamaica, 1660. [IRO][Birmingham City Library, Lyttleton ms 352032]

MIGNOT, ELIZABETH CROASDAILE, daughter of David Mignot MD in Kingston, Jamaica, married Henry Collick, son of William Collick of Shripney, Sussex, in London on 13 October 1846. [GM.ns27.79]

MILBERRY, JEFFREY, a planter in Jamaica, probate, 1678, PCC

MILBOURNE, THOMAS, in Vere parish, Jamaica, deeds, 1807-1809. [Cumberland Record Office]

MILES, WILLIAM JOHN, in Jamaica, accounts, 1759-1761. [Bristol Record Office, 11109]

MILLER, RICHARD, born 1753, a cooper from London, bound via London aboard the Capel for Jamaica in 1774. [TNA.T47.9/11]

MILLER, WILLIAM, from Jamaica, died in London on 8 March 1837. [GM.ns7.443]

113

MILLISON, GABRIEL, a mariner from Wapping, London, died in Port Royal, Jamaica, probate, 1698, PCC

MILLS, REBECCA, born 1692, died in St Elizabeth's, Jamaica, in December 1804. [GM.75.1171]

MILLS, THOMAS, born 1746, a carpenter from London, bound via London aboard the Northside Planter for Jamaica in 1774. [TNA.T47.9/11]

MILLS, Miss, daughter of James Mills in Jamaica, married Baron Lorentz, in London in December 1825. [GM.95.660]

MILLWARD, JOHN GARDNER, Lieutenant General of the Militia in Jamaica, died in Spanish Town on 24 December 1822. [GM.93.382]

MILLWARD, THOMAS NIXON, born 1789, died in Kingston, Jamaica, in 1819. [GM.89.177]

MILLWARD, T., from Jamaica, died in Gosfield Hall, Jamaica, on 12 October 1835. [GM.ns4,536]

MILLWARD, Miss, daughter of John Gardner Millward in Spanish Town, Jamaica, married Francis Rigby Brodbelt,, in Spanish Town on 25 July 1835. [GM,74.277]

MILNE, ANDREW, a merchant from Thaves Inn, died aboard the Augustus Caesar bound for Jamaica on 6 January 1804. [GM.74.182]

MILNE, JAMES ALEXANDER, born 1783, son of Mr Milne in London, died in Kingston, Jamaica, on 13 May 1808. [GM.78.655]

MILNE, PETER, born 1746, a tailor from London, bound via London aboard the Charming Sally for Jamaica in 1774. [TNA.T47.9/11]

MILNE, Mrs SOPHIA, from the Pedro River, Jamaica, died in Paris on 17 September 1822. [GM.92.649]

THE PEOPLE OF JAMAICA, 1655 TO 1855

MINOS, GEORGE, Custos of Portland, died in Port Antonio, Jamaica, on 6 January 1801. [GM.71.371]

MIRANDA, ABRAHAM, probate, 1748, Jamaica. [BM.Add.ms 21,931]

MITCHELL, CHARLES, born in 1758, from Jamaica, died in London on 18 April 1808. [GM.78.464]

MITCHELL, DAVID, born 1738, a merchant from London, via London aboard the Lady's Adventure bound for Jamaica in 1776. [TNA.T47.9/11]

MITCHELL, HUGH, a surgeon from Jamaica, died in Edinburgh on 22 July 1799. [GM.69.718]

MITCHELL, JAMES, the Receiver General of Jamaica, died in Spanish Town in August 1806. [GM.76.1075]

MITCHELL, JOHN, from London, died in Jamaica on 10 April 1815. [GM.85.646]

MITCHELL, JOHN, born 1812, son of Rowland Smith in London, died in Jamaica on 1 August 1840. [GM.ns14.676]

MITCHELL, JOHN, died 27 August 1840. [Kingston gravestone, Jamaica]

MODD, GEORGE, born 1679, died 14 July 1724, husband of Margaret, parents of Ann, born 7 August 1718, died 5 August 1724, Mary, born 14 January 1714, died 10 December 1719, and George, born 6 February 1713. St John's gravestone, Jamaica]

MODYFORD, Sir CHARLES, from London, died in Jamaica, probate, 1689, PCC

MOHUN, JOHN, a merchant in Jamaica, 1672. [IRO.Deeds.V.1/2]

MOIRE, WILLIAM, in Sea Lane, Port Royal, 1679. [IRO.Deeds.x.100]

THE PEOPLE OF JAMAICA, 1655 TO 1855

MOLESWORTH, Colonel HENDER, Governor of Jamaica, 8 July 1689. [CSP.VIII.234]

MONRO, CHARLES, born 1756, a bookkeeper from London, bound via London aboard the Capel bound for Jamaica in 1774. [TNA.T47.9/11]

MONROE, DUNCAN, a gentleman, emigrated via Portsmouth aboard the Richmond bound for Jamaica in 1775. [TNA.T47.9/11]

MONSANTO, ESTHER M., in Jamaica, probate, 1795, PCC

MONTAGUE, CHARLES WILLIAM, from Jamaica, died in England in 1820. [GM.90.379]

MONTAGUE, EDWARD, in Savanna la Mar, Jamaica, died in 1768. [GM.38.302]

MONTAGUE, MATTHEW, born 1768, from Black River, Jamaica, died on 17 March 1816. [GM.86.375]

MONTEATH, AMELIA, born 1767, widow of James Monteath in Jamaica, died in Lympstone, Devon, on 20 April 1833. [GM.103.476]

MONTEATH, ANDREW, a carpenter, died in Falmouth, Jamaica, on 11 June 1797. [GM.67.800]

MONTOYA, MARY JOSEPHINE, born 1819, died 4 October 1826. [Spring Path gravestone, Kingston, Jamaica]

MOODY, JOHN, born 1753, a millwright from Paddington, via London aboard the Princess Carolina bound for Jamaica in 1774. [TNA.T47.9/11]

MOORE, ALEXANDER JAMES, from Jamaica, married Sarah Hook, daughter of Richard Hook in Heathfield, Sussex, in London on 9 November 1840. [GM.ns13.85]

MOORE, DANIEL, born 1798, son of Daniel Moore in Jamaica, died on 19 January 1816. [GM.86.186]

MOORE, JOHN, born 1682, died 17 July 1733, husband of Prudence, born 1646, died 8 October 1733. [Chapleton, gravestone, Clarendon, Jamaica]

MOORE, WILLIAM, from Ireland, emigrated via Liverpool to Jamaica in 1698. [LRO]

MORALES, CHRISTOPHER BOYD MCLARTY, born 1842, Speaker in Jamaica, drowned on passage to England on 17 May 1864. [GM.ns2/17.120]

MORANT, CATHERINE, daughter of John Morant in Brackenhurst, Hampshire, died in Jamaica on 26 April 1802. [GM.72.686]

MORGAN, HENRY, Governor of Jamaica, a letter, 1680. [Bodleian Library, ms. Rawlinson.D843.187]

MORGAN, HENRY RHODES, from Jamaica, married Eliza Dawson, daughter of James Dawson, in London on 10 December 1821. [GM.91.641]; he died in London on 4 January 1836. [GM.ns5.211]

MORGAN, MARY ANN, born 1765, from Surrey, bound via London aboard the Royal Charlotte for Jamaica in 1774. [TNA.T47.9/11]

MORGAN, R., from Jamaica, died in London on 30 January 1813. [GM.83.287]

MORRIS, Captain HERMAN B., from New Hampshire, died 1795, died 31 May 1814. [Spring Path, Kingston, gravestone, Jamaica]

MORRIS, KATHERINE ROBERTS, born 1825, daughter of Samuel Jackson Roberts, and wife of Mowbray Morris, died in London on 3 November 1857. [GM.ns2/3.689]

MORRIS, RACHAEL ANGLIN, born 1789, died 1814. [Montego Bay gravestone, Jamaica]

THE PEOPLE OF JAMAICA, 1655 TO 1855

MORSE, EDWARD, former Chief Justice in Senegambia, died in Jamaica in 1794. [GM.64.768]

MORTON, CHARLES, died 1796. [Montego Bay gravestone, Jamaica]

MORTON, DAVID, MD, born 1731, from Jamaica, died in London on 18 July 1812. [GM.82.93]

MORTON, Mrs MARY, born 1742, widow of C. Morton in Jamaica, died at Newington Butts on 11 October 1823. [GM.93.180]

MOSELY, JOHN, a clerk in Port Royal, Jamaica, 1672, [IRO.Deeds.v.78]; a planter in 1673, [IRO.Deeds.v.254]; a mariner from Lothbury, London, died in Jamaica, probate, 1685, PCC

MOTRAL, THOMAS, born 1749, a servant from Norwich, bound via London aboard the St James to Jamaica in 1775. [TNA.T47.9/11]

MOWATT, WILLIAM, died in Jamaica in 1790. [GM.60.476]

MOWBRAY, HENRY, from Wapping, London, master of the Eastland Merchant died in Jamaica, probate, 1692, PCC

MUNDAY, EDWARD, a merchant from London, died in Jamaica aboard the Elizabeth, probate 1686, PCC

MUNN, DAVID, son of Captain James Munn in Ulverston, died in Gibbons, Vere, Clarendon, Jamaica, in 1793. [GM.63.1055]

MUNT, ISAAC, born 1759, died 4 February 1820. [Kingston gravestone, Jamaica]

MUNT, JUDITH, born 1762, widow of Isaac Munt in Kingston, Jamaica, died in Cheshunt, Hertfordshire, on 17 July 1837. [GM.ns8.325]

MUNT, SARAH, daughter of Isaac Munt in Jamaica, married J. Early Cook, in Nunnery, Cheshunt, on 5 February 1820. [GM.90.272]

THE PEOPLE OF JAMAICA, 1655 TO 1855

MURCH, Mrs HENRY, daughter of William Jackson in St Dorothy's, Jamaica, died in Naples on 1 March 1847. [GM.ns27.566]

MURCOTT, ISAAC BARNES, born 1812, son of Mr Murcott in Hinckley, a physician in Jamaica from 1840 to 1850, died 24 October 1850. [GM.ns35.222]

MURRAY, JOHN, [1], an American Loyalist, probably from South Carolina, who was granted land in St Elizabeth parish, Jamaica, in 1782. [TNA]

MURRAY, JOHN, [2], an American Loyalist, probably from South Carolina, who was granted land in St Elizabeth parish in 1782. [TNA]

MURRAY, PETER, from Jamaica, graduated MD from Edinburgh University in 1802. [EMG.33]

MURRAY, WALTER, born 1739, a gentleman returning to Jamaica aboard the Dawes via Portsmouth in 1775. [TNA.T47.9/11]

MUSGRAVE, NATHANIEL, fought at the Battle of Sedgemoor in Somerset, on 6 July 1685 against the forces of King James II, captured and transported from Portland Road aboard the Jamaican Merchant of London, master Charles Gardiner, bound for Jamaica in 1685.

MUSGRAVE, SIMON, Treasurer of the Society of Artillery of Jamaica, 1677. [IRO.Deeds.viii.103]; Attorney General, died in the earthquake of 1692. [JHR.VIII.60-62]

MYERS, Reverend JOHN MORRISON, a headmaster, died in Linstead, Spanish Town, Jamaica, on 2 February 1861. [GM.ns2/10.467]

MYERS, WILLIAM R., married Helen Spalding, daughter of Hinton Spalding MD, in Spanish Town, Jamaica, on 29 April 1845. [GM.ns24.189]; he died there on 9 April 1865. [GM.ns3/1.915]

MYRES, Misses, three ladies, emigrated via Portsmouth aboard the Richmond bound for Jamaica in 1775. [TNA.T47.9/11]

NAPIER, GEORGE, died in Whitehall, Clarendon, Jamaica, on 25 June 1806. [GM.76.874]

NARBONA, DAVID LOPEZ, probate, 1704

NASH, NICHOLAS, died in Jamaica, admin., 1657, PCC

NASMYTH, ISABELLA MAXWELL, daughter of Thomas Nasmyth MD in Jamaica, widow of Thomas Ryder, died at Hale End on 3 August 1832. [GM.102.188]

NASMYTH, MARY SABINA, daughter of Thomas Nasmyth in Jamaica, married Count Eduard de Melfort from Paris, in London on 11 January 1826. [GM.95.80]

NASMYTH, ROBERT, born 1798, son of Mrs Nasmyth in Jamaica, died in Toulouse on 7 January 1817. [GM.87.91]

NASMYTH, THOMAS, MD, died in Water Valley, Jamaica, on 9 June 1806. [GM.76.874]

NATHAN, ELIZA, daughter of J. P. Nathan in Jamaica, married Thomas Maitland Snow, a banker, son of Thomas Snow in Franklin, Littleham, on 27 February 1851. [GM.ns35.424]

NATHAN, EMILY, daughter of J. P. Nathan in Trelawney, Jamaica, married Captain Rocke of the 2nd Queen's Royal Regiment, in Exmouth on 27 June 1850. [GM.ns34.320]

NATHAN, J. P., from Portsmouth, died in Jamaica on 25 October 1831. [GM.102.94]

NATTRIS, ISAAC, died in Jamaica, admin., 1656, PCC

NEEDHAM, HENRY, in Jamaica, died 1758. [GM.28.94]

NELSON, JOHN, died in St Mary's, Jamaica, in 1800. [GM.70.905]

THE PEOPLE OF JAMAICA, 1655 TO 1855

NETHERSOLE, ELIZA, daughter of John Nethersole in Jamaica, married William Cunningham Glen, a barrister, in London on 15 December 1848. [GM.ns31.200]

NETHERWOOD, JOSEPH, born 1755, a clerk from London, via London aboard the Princess Carolina bound for Jamaica in 1774. [TNA.T47.9/11]

NETTLEFOLD, JOHN, a planter, died at Martha Brae, Jamaica, on 29 June 1798. [GM.68.811]

NEUFVILLE, JACOB, of Lymington, Hampshire, and Jamaica, died in Manchioneal, Jamaica, in 1817. [GM.87.637]; his widow Sybylla Phoebe, died in Lee on 14 November 1811. [GM.101.475]

NEWMAN, CHARLES, from New Fish Street, London, died in Jamaica, probate, 1693, PCC

NEWMAN, HENRY, son of T. Harding Newman in Helmes, Essex, died at Montego Bay in 1846. [GM.ns25.335]

NEWSTEAD, ROBERT, born 1747, a husbandman from Somerlyton in Suffolk, bound aboard the Norfolk via Yarmouth for Jamaica in 1775. [TNA.T47.9/11]

NEWTON, ISAAC, a factor in Jamaica in 1673. [IRO.Deeds.i.213]

NIBBS, J. G., in St Anne's, Jamaica, died in London in 1823. [GM.93.188]

NICHOLDS, WILLIAM, a blacksmith on HMS Success died in Port Royal, Jamaica, probate, 1692, PCC

NIXON, JOHN, a Judge of the Supreme Court, Colonel of Militia, and an Assemblyman in Jamaica, died on 15 April 1774. [GM.44.287]

NORERO, ELIAS, a merchant in Port Royal, 1684. [IRO.Deeds.xxi.31]

THE PEOPLE OF JAMAICA, 1655 TO 1855

NOSEWORTHY, THOMAS, a gentleman in Jamaica in 1670. [IRO.Deeds.iii.229]

NOWELL, Mrs, widow of J. Nowell in Jamaica, died in Southampton in 1814. [GM.84.95]

NUGENT, Sir GEORGE, Governor of Jamaica, 1801-1802, 1802-1805, papers. Royal United Service Institution, [MM3, and MM183A-D]; a son was born at Government Pen, Jamaica, on 12 October 1802. [GM.72.1159]; a daughter was born on 8 September 1803. [GM.73.1084]

NUGENT, RICHARD, born 1754, a gentleman from Surrey, bound via London aboard the Royal Charlotte for Jamaica in 1774. [TNA.T47.9/11]

NUNES, CORDOZO ISAAC, probate, 1741, Jamaica. [BM.Add.ms 21,931]

NUNEZ, ISAAC, in Jamaica, petitioned the Council for Trade and Plantations in London, on 30 August 1692. [JCTP]

NUNEZ, ISAAC R., in Jamaica, probate, 1793, PCC

NUNEZ, Reverend MAXIMILIAN, son of John Nunez in Jamaica, married Catherine Kendal, daughter of Henry Kendal, in London on 7 June 1859. [GM.ns2/9.81]

NUNES, WILLIAM GEORGE, Commissioner for Stamps, died in Jamaica on 4 April 1854. [GM.ns42.90]

OAKE, MICHAEL, a bachelor in Port Royal, Jamaica, probate, 1699, PCC

OATES, GEORGE HIBBERT, son of Mrs Oates in Bath, died in Jamaica on 11 April 1837. [GM.ns8.326]

OATES, HIBBERT, born 1796, son of Mr Oates on Sion Hill, Bath, died in Kingston, Jamaica, on 14 December 1840. [GM.ns15.558]

O'BRYEN, JAMES, in Port Royal, Jamaica, probate, 1694, PCC

THE PEOPLE OF JAMAICA, 1655 TO 1855

O'BRYNE, ADAM, born 1749, a gentleman from London, bound via London aboard the Ashley for Jamaica in 1774. [TNA.T47.9/11]

O'CONNOR, CHARLES, of Charlemount, born 1771, died 4 March 1839. [Montego Bay gravestone, Jamaica]

OGILVIE, DUNCAN, an American Loyalist, probably from South Carolina, who was granted land in St Elizabeth parish, Jamaica, in 1782. [TNA]

OGLE, JAMES, a bricklayer in Jamaica, his will and business papers, 1714-1724. [Lincoln Archives. Ancaster.9.A.4]

O'KEEFE, Reverend T., chaplain to the Duke of Clarence, son of Mr O'Keefe the celebrated writer, died in Jamaica in 1805. [GM.75.677]

OLDHAM, WILLIAM, a merchant in Jamaica, died on 18 June 1800. [GM.70.798]

OLIPHANT, Dr David, a planter in Jamaica, 1789. [TNA.AO13.88.96-104]

OLIVER, GEORGE, a magistrate in Craigmill, Jamaica, died in London on 22 August 1818. [GM.88.378]

OLIVER, JOSEPH, in Jamaica, 27 September 1688. [TNA.Prob.4/20544]

ONIONS, JOHN, a merchant in Port Royal, Jamaica, probate, 1685, PCC

ORD, JAMES, a planter of 170 acres in St Andrew's parish, Jamaica, in 1754. [TNA.CO137/28/171-196]

ORD, Sir JOHN, late Governor of Jamaica, married Miss Frere, daughter of James Frere in London, on 3 December 1793. [GM.63.1148]

O'REILLY, DOWELL, born 1795, son of Matthew O'Reilly in Knock Castle, County Louth, the Attorney General of Jamaica, died in St

Andrew's, Kingston, Jamaica, on 13 September 1855.
[GM.ns24.651]

O'REILLY, RICHARD, Judge of the Supreme Court of Jamaica, died
in Kingston, Jamaica, on 22 December 1860. [GM.ns2/10.348]

ORGILL, CHARLES RICHARD, of Portland, Jamaica, married Harriet
Davies, daughter of Reverend John Davies of Pedworth, Berkshire,
in Salisbury in 1800. [GM.70.1284]

ORR, CHARLESIANNA, widow of Bryan Orr of Castle Estate,
Portland, Jamaica, died in London on 26 September 1820.
[GM.90.377]

ORSETT, GEORGE, Assemblyman for Kingston, died in Jamaica in
1845. [GM.ns24.665]

OSBORN, Reverend DANIE, born 1812, St George's, Jamaica, died
at sea on 27 February 1853. [GM.ns39.558]

PAFFORD, JOHN, a bricklayer of Goose Creek and Hampstead Hill,
Charleston, a Loyalist who moved to Jamaica in 1783.
[TNA.AO12.100.294, etc]

PAGE, MOSES, from Southwark, London, a mariner aboard the
Jamaica Factor, died in Jamaica, probate,1676, PCC

PAGE, WILLIAM, fought at the Battle of Sedgemoor in Somerset,
on 6 July 1685 against the forces of King James II, captured and
transported from Portland Road aboard the Jamaican Merchant of
London, master Charles Gardiner, bound for Jamaica in 1685.

PAISE, WILLIAM, from Chatham, died in Jamaica, admin., 1656,
PCC

PAISLEY, SARAH ANNE, daughter of W. Paisley, married Reverend
Ewan James, from London, in Jamaica on 15 October 1818.
[GM.88.370]

PALMER, CHARLES N., married Mrs Ingoldsby Massey, from
Norbiton, Surrey, in Jamaica on 2 June 1808. [GM.78.556]

THE PEOPLE OF JAMAICA, 1655 TO 1855

PALMER, HENRY, in Jamaica, 12 May 1684. [TNA.Prob.4.898]

PALMER, JAMES, in Bristol, Jamaica, died at Hot Wells on 5 July 1806. [GM.76.777]

PALMEUR, JOHN, a gentleman, emigrated via Portsmouth aboard the Richmond bound for Jamaica in 1775. [TNA.T47.9/11]

PALMER, JOHN, son of John Palmer in Wiltshire Park, Clarendon, Jamaica, died in Becklington on 18 February 1825. [GM.95.381]

PALMER, J., born 1742, from Jamaica, died in Bath in 1819. [GM.88.92]

PALMER, MARY, born 1787, daughter of Mr Gatfield in London, wife of H. Palmer in the Green Mountains, died in Jamaica on 12 December 1810. [GM.81.293]

PALMER, Mrs ROSA, died 1 May 1790. [Montego Bay gravestone, Jamaica]

PALMER, SARAH, born 1728, widow of Henry John Palmer in Jamaica, died in Bath on 2 August 1814. [GM.84.198]

PANTON, ANNIS RACHEL, daughter of Reverend Panton in Widcombe, niece of the Vice Chancellor of Jamaica, married Mayow Short, Chairman of the Quarter Sessions, in Jamaica on 15 June 1847. [GM.ns28.311]

PANTON, ELIZA, in Manchioneal, married J. D. Andrews in Port Antonio, Jamaica, in 1800. [GM.70.1283]

PANTON, Reverend RICHARD, Archdeacon of Surrey, Jamaica, died on 30 August 1860. [GM.ns2/9.438]

PAPLAY, Miss, married William Hey the Customs Commissioner, in Jamaica on 5 April 1783. [GM.53.363]

PARDO, JEOSUAH HISQUIAU, was born in Amsterdam in 1626, settled in Curacao from 1647 to 1683, then moved to Jamaica.

THE PEOPLE OF JAMAICA, 1655 TO 1855

PARKE, MARY, youngest daughter of William Parke of The Thicketts, Jamaica, married Reverend H. Morland Austen of Crayford, Kent, in Sturminster, Dorset, on 15 September 1853. [GM.NS40.628]

PARKE, WILLIAM, a merchant in Kingston, Jamaica, papers, 1703-1706. [Lincoln Archives, Monson.28.b.5]

PARKE, WILLIAM, in Kingston, Jamaica, papers, 1803-1809. [Lancashire Record Office, DDCh]

PARKER, GEORGE, son of John Parker, a planter in Jamaica, died in London on 1 October 1788. [GM.58.936]

PARKER, HENRY, from Jamaica, died in London on 9 November 1787. [GM.57.1031]

PARKER, ISABEL, widow of Henry Parker in Jamaica, married James Grierson in London in 1788. [GM.58.269]

PARKER, JOSEPH, a merchant in Port Royal, Jamaica, probate, 1676, PCC

PARKER, PAUL, born 1757, a merchant from London, from London aboard the Lady's Adventure bound for Jamaica in 1776. [TNA.T47.9/11]

PARKER, THOMAS, born 1761, from Jamaica, died in London on 3 April 1823. [GM.93.382]

PARKER, Lieutenant Colonel WILLIAM, in Port Royal, 1683. [IRO.Deeds.xv.39]

PARNELL, T. O., born 1801, son of T. O. Parnell in Warminster, died in Jamaica on 19 September 1829. [GM.99.651]

PARRIS, JOHN, a merchant in Jamaica, 1671. [IRO.Deeds.iii.227]

PARRY, HENRY, of Leyden Estate, Montego Bay, Jamaica, died in Northrop, Flintshire, on 18 January 1820. [GM.90.187]

PARTRIDGE, THOMAS, an estate owner in Jamaica, died 12 May 1759. [GM.29.242]

PARTRIDGE, THOMAS, from London, died in Jamaica in 1820. [GM.90.379]

PATTERSON, MARIAN, daughter of William Patterson in Jamaica, married Charles Vardon in Battersea, Surrey, on 15 May 1806. [GM.76.477]

PATTINSON, WILLIAM, a merchant, died in Jamaica in 1791. [GM.61.1065]

PATTISON, MARY, daughter of Dr Robert Pattison in Water Valley, Jamaica, married Reverend Thomas Barry Cahusal, on 1 May 1845. [GM.ns24.189]

PAGAGEAU, Mrs M. L., born 1744, died 21 October 1812

PATEY, B. C., born 1780, a merchant, died 26 January 1837. [Kingston gravestone, Jamaica]

PEACOCKE, SANDFORD, and his wife Amelia, with estates in Jamaica, 1804. [Northampton, Wykes ms.Ah.242]

PEALE, ELIJAH, late in Jamaica, 7 October 1684. [TNA.Prob.4.20480]

PEARSON, THOMAS, a merchant in London and commander of the ship Seven Oaks, died in Port Royal, Jamaica, probate, 1684, PCC

PEEKE, JOHN, in Port Royal, 1677. [IRO.Deeds.viii.87]

PELL, BARTOLEMEW, died in Jamaica, 1698. [TNA.Prob.5.5987]

PELLATORY, GARRETT, died in Jamaica, admin., 1657, PCC

PENNANT, EDWARD, born 1672, Chief Justice, Custos Rotulorum of Clarendon and Vere, died 11 June 1736. [Clarendon gravestone, Jamaica]; husband of Elizabeth, born 1689, died 13 January 1735. [Chapleton gravestone, Clarendon, Jamaica]

THE PEOPLE OF JAMAICA, 1655 TO 1855

PENNOCK, ELIZA, daughter of John Pennock in Kingston, Jamaica, and wife of Mr Hanson in London, died 19 June 1820. [GM.90.638]

PEREIRA, ABIGAIL, in Jamaica, probate, 1798, PCC

PEREIRA, BENJAMIN MENDES, in Jamaica, probate, 1802, PCC

PEREIRA, DANIEL, probate, 1748, Jamaica. [BM.Add.ms 21,931]

PEREIRA, ISAAC MENDES, in Jamaica, probate, 1793, PCC

PEREIRA, MENASSAH, probate, 1741, Jamaica. [BM. Add. Ms 21,931]

PEREIRA, SARAH, probate, 1750, Jamaica. [BM.Add.ms 21,931]

PERRIN, WILLIAM, in Jamaica, died in 1759. [GM.29.293]

PERRY, ALEXANDER, born 1749, a tailor from London, bound via London aboard the Charming Sally for Jamaica in 1774. [TNA.T47.9/11]

PERRY, ANN, born 1755, from Wolverhampton, bound via London aboard the Fanny for Jamaica in 1774. [TNA.T47.9/11]

PERRY, ANNE, daughter of John Perry, died at Montego Bay, Jamaica, on 29 December 1809. [GM.10.283]

PERRY, ELIZABETH, daughter of John Perry from Bristol, died at Montego Bay, Jamaica, on 5 January 1806. [GM.76.281]

PERRY, ELIZABETH CHARLOTTE, from Bristol, wife of William Perry, died in Jamaica on 26 December 1814. [GM.85.179]

PERRY, JOHN, born 1751, an Assemblyman and Judge of the Common Pleas Court of Jamaica, died there on 10 April 1809, [Montego Bay gravestone, Jamaica][GM.79.984]

PETERKIN, ALEXANDER, a gentleman, emigrated via Portsmouth aboard the Richmond bound for Jamaica in 1775. [TNA.T47.9/11]

PETERS, CHARLES, born 1799, died 22 December 1814. [Spring Path, Kingston, gravestone, Jamaica]

PHELPES, ..., died in Jamaica, administration, 1659, PCC

PHILIBERT, JOHN BAPTIST, born 1796, died 7 January 1842. [Spring Path gravestone, Kingston, Jamaica]

PHILIBERT, SARAH ANTONETTE, born 1803, died 18 December 1811. [Spring Path gravestone, Kingston, Jamaica]

PHILLIPS, ANNA, widow of Samuel Phillips in Portsmouth, died in Jamaica on 7 November 1831. [GM.102.94]

PHILLIPS, Reverend EBENEZER, a Baptist missionary, died in Jamaica on 12 October 1825. [GM.95.575]; Elizabeth, his widow, died in Jamaica on 15 October 1825. [GM.95.575]

PHILLIPS, NATHANIEL, in Jamaica, records,1759-1792. [NLW.Slebech papers]; probate, 1766, PCC

PHILLIPS, ROBERT, a sailmaker in Port Royal, 1677. [IRO.Deeds.viii.186]

PHILLIPS, Captain ROBERT, died 1702. [St Andrew's gravestone, Jamaica]

PHILLIPS, ROBERT, in Jamaica, died 1764. [GM.34.46]

PHILLIPS, THOMAS, born 1775, harbourmaster at Annotto Bay, died 18 August 1822. [Annotto Bay gravestone, Jamaica]

PHILPOT, JOHN, a gunsmith in Port Royal, 1680. [IRO.Deeds.xi.106]

PHIPPS, PAUL, an Assemblyman, judge, and Colonel of Militia of St Andrew's, died in Kingston, Jamaica, in October 1787. [GM.57.1194]

PHIPPS, PAUL, from Kingston, Jamaica, died aboard the Grantham Packet on passage to England in 1788. [GM.58.1181]; his widow, Sarah, died on 9 February 1820. [GM.90.282]

PICKERING, WILLIAM, a shipwright from Aldgate, London, died in Jamaica, probate, 1690, PCC

PICTERNELLE, Miss CORNELIA BROOK, born in Curacao, died 17 July 1826. [Spring Path gravestone, Kingston, Jamaica]

PILKINGTON, JOHN EDWARD, son of Major Pilkington, died in Jamaica on 24 February 1841. [GM.ns16.111]

PINHORNE, EDWARD, in Jamaica, dead by 1669. [IRO.Deeds.iii.38]

PINNOCK, GRACE, daughter of George Pinnock, died in Jamaica on 2 February 1818. [GM.88.568]

PINNOCK, GRACE ELIZABETH, daughter of Phillip Pinnock in Jamaica, married John Milbourne Augustus Marsh, son of J. M. Marsh the Postmaster General of Jamaica, in London on 26 January 1848. [GM.ns29.422]

PINNOCK, JAMES, a barrister in Jamaica, diary, 1758-1794, and accounts, 1758 – 1810. [BM. Newcastle. Add.33316, 33317]

PINNOCK, JAMES, and Mary, parents of James Pinnock, born 1713, died 20 June 1736. [St Andrew's gravestone, Jamaica]

PINNOCK, PHILIP, from Jamaica, died in London on 5 January 1817. [GM.87.91]

PINNOCK, SAMUEL, born 1671, died in Kingston, Jamaica, in 1796. [GM.66.615]

PINNOCK, Mrs, born 1757, widow of J. Pinnock of London and Jamaica, died in Southampton on 23 November1836. [GM.ns7.108]

PINTO, JOSEPH, probate, 1733, Jamaica. [BM.Add.ms21,931]

PLANTER, WILLIAM, died in Jamaica in 1791. [GM.61.682]

PLAYFORD, ARTHUR, son of Henry Playford of Northrepps, Norfolk, died in Jamaica on 30 October 1851. [GM.ns37.208]

THE PEOPLE OF JAMAICA, 1655 TO 1855

PLEYDELL, JOHN, a merchant, son of Samuel Pleydell MD in Jamaica, died in Edinburgh on 23 March 1807. [GM.77.385]

PLUMMER, JOHN, died in Jamaica, admin., 1657, PCC

PLUMMER, JOHN, of Rotherhithe, Surrey, purser aboard HMS Falcon, died in Port Royal, Jamaica, probate, 1688, PCC

PLUMMER, WILLIAM, jr., born 1772, died in St James, Jamaica, on 10 January 1801. [GM.71.372]

POLLOCK, Mrs CHARLOTTE, an American Loyalist, probably from South Carolina, who was granted land in St Elizabeth parish, Jamaica, in 1782. [TNA]

POLLOCK, HUGH, a saddler in Charleston, S.C., husband of Charlotte Pollock, moved to Jamaica in 1778, died there in 1782. [TNA.AO12.99.336, etc]

POOLE, Reverend THOMAS, in Clarendon, Jamaica, died 1791. [GM.61.682]

POPHAM, Miss, daughter of Sir Home Popham, died in Jamaica in March 1820. [GM.90.568]

POPKIN, WILLIAM BASSETT, born 1788, son of John Popkin in Talygren, Glamorgan, settled in Jamaica in 1822, died at Montego Bay in 1845. [GM.ns23.679]

PORTELLO, MOSES, probate, 1748, Jamaica. [BM.Add.ms21,931]

PORTEOUS, JAMES, born 1809, Councillor of Jamaica, and Custos of St Andrew's, Jamaica, died in London on 5 October 1861. [GM.ns2/11.692]

POSSON, ANTHONY COLE, from Liverpool, died in Kingston, Jamaica, in 1793. [GM.63.1152]

POTLE, MATHEW, fought at the Battle of Sedgemoor in Somerset, on 6 July 1685 against the forces of King James II, captured and transported from Portland Road aboard the Jamaican Merchant of London, master Charles Gardiner, bound for Jamaica in 1685.

POVEY, R., in Jamaica, a letter, 1664. [Bodleian, ms. Clarendon.82 ff253-258]

POWELL, JOHN, born 1750, an accountant, via Bristol aboard the Egale bound for Jamaica in 1775. [TNA.T47.9/11]

POWELL, MARY, born 1741, from London, bound via London aboard the Dawes for Jamaica in 1774. [TNA.T47.9/11]

POWELL, THOMAS, born 1759, returning to Jamaica via London aboard the Catherine for Jamaica in 1774. [TNA.T47.9/11]

POWELL, Mrs, widow of Thomas Powell, from Henley Grove, Westbury, died in Bellynure, Jamaica, in November 1843. [GM.ns21.334]

POWNALL, JAMES CORNE, died in Kingston, Jamaica, on 4 September 1825. [GM.95.478]

PRATT, ROSELLA, born 1796, died 10 November 1844. [Spring Path, Kingston, gravestone, Jamaica]

PRATT, THOMAS, died in Jamaica in 1791. [GM.61.1065]

PRICE, Colonel CHARLES, born 1678, died 23 May 1730, and his wife Sarah Edmunds, parents of Deborah, 1714-1716, Katherine, 1710-1717, Elizabeth, 1705-1717, Francis, 1720-1720, Sarah, 1707-1721, Deborah, 1716-1721, Phillip, 1722-1722, Elizabeth Katherine, 1718-1727, Charles, Thomas, John. [St John's gravestone, Jamaica]

PRICE, Sir CHARLES, died in Jamaica in 1772. [GM.42.542]

PRICE, Sir CHARLES, Major General of the Militia, Assemblyman for St Thomas in the Vale, a magistrate for St Catherine's, died in Spanish Town, Jamaica, on 18 October 1788. [GM.59.178]

PRICE, EMILY VALENTINA, daughter of Edward, Lord Dunsany, wife of George Price, died in Ellerslie, Jamaica, on 30 September 1864. [GM.ns2/17.798]

PRICE, GEORGE, born 1803, from Bennett's Bridge, County Kilkenny, died on Tulloch Estate, Jamaica, on 15 April 1848. [GM.ns30.110]

PRIESTLEY, THOMAS, from Jamaica, married Henrietta Carteret, from Gloucester, on 18 October 1767. [GM.37.523]

PRINCE, JOHN, in Port Royal, Jamaica, probate, 1700. [Bristol Record Office, 0458/13]

PRINCE, LAWRENCE, a landowner in Liguana, Jamaica, 1679. [IRO.Deeds.liber i.129]

PRINCE, Mrs M., wife of Thomas Prince jr., in Jamaica, granddaughter of Sir Christopher Hales, died in Portland, Jamaica, on 1 November 1807. [GM.78.86]

PRINCE, MARY ANNE, born 1803, daughter of T. Prince of Jamaica and Bath, died in Jamaica on 3 July 1826. [GM.96.191]

PRINCE, THOMAS, jr., in Jamaica, married Marianne Sanderson, the niece of Sir John Hales of Blashford, Hampshire, in London on 31 October 1803. [GM.73.1254]

PRINGLE, JAMES, born 1758, a gentleman from London, bound via London aboard the Dawes for Jamaica in 1774. [TNA.T47.9/11]

PRINGLE, JOHN, an American Loyalist, probably from South Carolina, who was granted land in St Elizabeth parish, Jamaica, in 1782. [TNA]

PRINGLE, JOHN ALEXANDER GORDON, born 1833, of the 3rd West Indian Regiment, son of Mark Pringle in Oakenden, Sussex, died in Jamaica on 31 July 1853. [GM.ns40.426]

PRIOLEAU, PHILIP, born 1715, settled in Jamaica before 1742, died there in 1790. [GM.60.1148]

PROBY, SAMUEL, a citizen and merchant tailor of London, died in Jamaica, probate, 1680, PCC

PUGH, PETER, in Jamaica, dead by 1671. [IRO.Deeds.iii.227]

PURDIGO, FRANCIS, born 1632 in Greece, died 1742 in Jamaica. [GM.13.443]

PUSEY, WILLIAM, born 1741, Assemblyman for St Dorothy's, died 11 June 1783, husband of Elizabeth Rule, born 174-, died 8 June 178-. [St Dorothy gravestone, Jamaica]

PYE, GEORGE, a mariner from Rotherhithe Wall, Surrey, died in Port Royal, Jamaica, probate, 1685, will, 1686, PCC

QUENEBOROUGH, SAMUEL, formerly an Assemblyman fo St John's, Jamaica, died in Dunstable on 13 October 1815. [GM.85.382]

QUIXANO, MENDES ABRAHAM, probate, 1738, Jamaica. [BM.Add.ms 21,931]

QUIXANO, MENDES DAVID, probate, 1738, Jamaica. [BM.Add.ms.21,931]

RABB, NICHOLAS, born 1772, died 11 November 1833. [Kingston gravestone, Jamaica]

RAINFORD, SAMUEL, a merchant in Kingston, Jamaica, papers,1766 to 1809. [Lancashire Record Office, DDCh]; born in Cheshire in 1716, a merchant, died 30 July 1798. [Kingston gravestone, Jamaica]

RAINFORD, Captain JAMES, born 1702, from Liverpool, died 21 November 1734. [Kingston gravestone, Jamaica]

RAINFORD, Captain, a merchant from Liverpool, with his wife and children, bound aboard the Mary via Liverpool to Jamaica in 1774. [TNA.T47.9/11]

RAITT, ANDREW, a planter of 60 acres in St Andrew's parish, Jamaica, in 1754. [TNA.CO137/28/171-196]

RAM, JOSEPH, born 1669, died in Jamaica in December 1809. [GM.79.277]

RAMSAY, ALLAN, an American Loyalist, probably from South Carolina, who was granted land in St Elizabeth parish, Jamaica, in 1782. [TNA]

RAMSAY, GEORGE, an American Loyalist, probably from South Carolina, who was granted land in St Elizabeth parish, Jamaica, in 1782. [TNA]

RAMSAY, PETER, born 1733, Registrar in Chancery, died 27 October 1781. [St Catherine's gravestone, Jamaica]

RAMSAY, ..., daughter of William Ramsay in Jamaica, was born in Hanwell, Middlesex, on 10 October 1806. [GM.76.977]

RAND, WILLIAM, born 1710, died 18 September 1760. [Chapleton gravestone, Clarendon, Jamaica]

RANKIN, GEORGE, died in Jamaica in 1791. [GM.61.1065]

RAVENCAMP, FREDERICK, of Mooures Park, married Miss Ingram, daughter of Peter Ingram former Provost Marshal of Jamaica, in St George's, Jamaica, in October 1789. [GM.60.83]

READE, Colonel, died in the earthquake of 1692. [JHR.viii.60-62]

REDWAR, JOHN, a planter in Jamaica, 1670. [IRO.Deeds.iii.33]

REDWOOD, PHILIP, born 1750, formerly the Chief Justice in Jamaica, and Speaker of the Jamaica Assembly, died in London in 1810. [GM.80.287]

THE PEOPLE OF JAMAICA, 1655 TO 1855

REED, JAMES, born 1747, a tailor from London, via London aboard the Lady Tuliana bound for Jamaica in 1774. [TNA.T47.9/11]

REED, JOHN, a mariner from Plymouth, died in Jamaica, probate, 1686, PCC

REEVES, ...,Provost Marshal, died in the earthquake of 1692. [JHR.viii.60-62]

REID, CAROLINE, daughter of E. James Reid in Saltpool, Spanish Town, married Joseph Dods in Stanford, Hornsey, on 31 May 1860. [GM.ns2/9.86]

REID, EDWARD MATTHEW, son of E. J. Reid in Jamaica, married Sarah Fenwick Bowen, only child of W. S. Bowen of Naseby Woolley, Northamptonshire, there on 6 October 1841. [GM.ns16.648]

REID, ELIZABETH, married Alexander Roberts, in Kingston, Jamaica, in 1800. [GM.70.483]

REID, JOHN LYNCH, of Queen's College, Cambridge, and John's Hall, Brown Town, Jamaica, married Christianna Robey, daughter of J. W. Robey of Kentish Town, in London on 15 July 1848. [GM.ns30.316]

REID, LOUISA ELIZABETH, daughter of George Reid in Jamaica, married Reverend John Louis Petit, in Rye, Kent, on 5 June 1828. y

REID, Mrs REBECCA, wife of Colonel Thomas Reid, born 1723, died 11 April 1747. [Golden Grove Estate gravestone, Jamaica]

REID, THOMAS, Major General of Militia, died 1793. Falmouth gravestone, Jamaica]

REID, WASHINGTON, a Captain if the United States Navy, died in Jamaica in March 1813. [GM.83.660]

RENNALLS, JOHN POWELL, from Jamaica, graduated MD from Edinburgh University in 1797. [EMG.28]; he, from Spanish Town, Jamaica, died in Clapton on 12 September 1813. [GM.83.402]

REYNOLDS, THOMAS, son of William Reynolds in Catherine Mount Estste, died in Jamaica on 1 March 1850. [GM.ns30.558]

RIBERO, ISAAC, probate, 1745, Jamaica. [BM. Add.ms21,931]

RICHARDS, ROBERT, from Carrickmacros, died in Kingston, Jamaica, in 1790. [GM.60.373]

RICHARDSON, JAMES, in Jamaica, died 1758. [GM.59.178]

RICHARDSON, JOHN, a servant to Sir Robert Modyford in the parish of St Ann, Jamaica, probate, 1683, PCC.

RICHARDSON, J. R., born 1811, died 21 November 1857. [St John's gravestone, Jamaica]

RICHARDSON, SAMUEL, a bricklayer in the Goat Pens, Port Royal, 1683. [IRO.Deeds.xvii.70]

RICKELL, CHARLES WILLIAM, born 1810, son of Joseph Rickell in Oudle, died in Falmouth, Jamaica, on 2 February 1853. [GM.ns39.560]

RICKETTS, JOHN CRAWFORD, born 1705, coachman to G. C. Ricketts the Attorney General of Jamaica, died in Spanish Town, Jamaica, in 1847. [GM.ns27.334]

RICKETTS, Mrs MARY, born 1738, widow of William Henry Ricketts in Canaan, Jamaica, mother of Viscount St Vincent, died in Bath on 12 March 1828. [GM.98.570]

RICKETTS, W. H., born 1754, a gentleman planter, from Southampton, bound for Jamaica via London aboard the Esther in 1773. [TNA.T47.9/11]; William Henry Ricketts, [jr.?], died in Jamaica on 30 June 1790. [GM.60.669]; William Henry Ricketts,

THE PEOPLE OF JAMAICA, 1655 TO 1855

from Longwood, Hampshire, Councillor, of Canaan, Westmoreland, Jamaica, died in Jamaica on 5 October1798. [GM.69.78]

RIENSETT, PETER, born 1755, died 5 August 1820, also his daughter Sarah Allen Jane the wife of Edward Campbell Woodgate, born1802, died 4 March 1837. [Kingston gravestone, Jamaica]

RILEY, JOHN, born 1753, a tavern waiter from London, via London aboard the Great Marlow bound for Jamaica in 1774. [TNA.T47.9/11]

RILEY, THOMAS, from St Anne's, Jamaica, died in Liverpool, on 23 January 1801. [GM.71.186]

RITCHIE, ALEXANDER, an attorney, died in Kingston, Jamaica, in April 1807. [GM.77.682]

RITCHIE, HELEN, born 1808, daughter of J. Ritchie, and wife of W. Heath of Spring Mount Estate Jamaica, died in Jamaica on 29 August 1841. [GM.ns16.668]

ROAFE, JOHN, died in Jamaica, admin., 1656, PCC

ROB, MARY PATTISON, daughter of Dr Rob in Water Valley, Jamaica, married Reverend Thomas Barry Cahusae, in Jamaica, on 1 May 1845. [GM.ns24.189]

ROBBINS, ALFRED EARLE, born 1804, died 18 May 1852. [Kingston gravestone, Jamaica]

ROBBINS, THOMAS, born in Tewkesbury, St Mary's, Jamaica, died in Jamaica on 29 December 1802. [GM.73.181]

ROBERTS, ALEXANDER, married Elizabeth Reid, in Kingston, Jamaica, in 1800. [GM.70.483]

ROBERTS, D. S., born 1781, a Major of the 54th Regiment, died 12 December 1829. [Kingston gravestone, Jamaica]

ROBERTS, WALTER, son of Samuel Roberts in Great Borzell, Sussex, died in Kingston, Jamaica, on 18 February 1813. [GM.83.660]

ROBERTS, WALTER, a Lieutenant of the 3rd West Indian Regiment, married Julia Mary De La Mere, daughter of P. Herbert De La Mere, Captain of the 3rd West Indian Regiment, in Kingston, Jamaica, on 6 July1857. [GM.ns3/2.383]

ROBERTSON, GEORGE, fought at the Battle of Sedgemoor in Somerset, on 6 July 1685 against the forces of King James II, captured and transported from Portland Road aboard the Jamaican Merchant of London, master Charles Gardiner, bound for Jamaica in 1685.

ROBERTSON, KATHERINE HALL, born 24 May 1801, died 1 April 1821. [Spring Path gravestone, Kingston]

ROBERTSON, MARY MARGARET ADAM, daughter of John Robertson in Belmont, Jamaica, married the Chevalier Thomas Francis Sargent, Chamberlain to the Duke of Lucca, in Paris on 29 May 1841. [GM.ns34.566]

ROBERTSON, ROBERT, a surgeon aboard the Siam, died in Jamaica, probate, 1693, PCC

ROBERTSON, ROBERT HENRY, son of Duncan Robertson in St Elizabeth's, Jamaica, married Elizabeth Frances Farquharson, daughter of Matthew Farquharson in St Elizabeth's, Jamaica in London on 19 March 1864. [GM.ns2/16.521]

ROBINSON, CHARLES, son of George Robinson in London, died on Copse Estate, Montego Bay, Jamaica, on 14 September1853. [GM.ns40.649]

ROBINSON, D., from England, died in Jamaica in 1791. [GM.61.187]

ROBINSON, GEORGE, from Jamaica, married Miss Mason, daughter of Reverend Edward Mason in Blyth, Nottinghamshire, on 10 February 1793. [GM.ns63.280]

ROBINSON, JEREMIAH, a barrister and recorder, died in Appleby, Westmoreland, Jamaica, on 21 January 1792. [GM.63.94]

ROCHFORT, Mrs ELIZABETH, born 1725, died 1783, wife of Dr Robert Rochford. [Montego Bay gravestone, Jamaica]

RODRIQUES, ABRAHAM, probate, 1733, Jamaica. [BM.Add.ms21,931]

RODRINGUER, DANIEL, probate, 1741, Jamaica. [BM.Add.ms21,931]

RODRIQUES, or CARDOZO, DAVID, probate, 1815, Jamaica.

ROLFE, MARY, born 1754, a servant from London, bound via London aboard the St James to Jamaica in 1775. [TNA.T47.9/11]

ROPER, MARY ANN, born 1799, died 25 April 1833. [Spring Path gravestone, Kingston, Jamaica]

ROSBURGH, ANTHONY, an American Loyalist, probably from South Carolina, who was granted land in St Elizabeth parish, Jamaica, in 1782. [TNA]

ROSE, FULKE, of St Catherine's, Jamaica, died in London, probate, 1694, PCC

ROSE, WINSTON ELIZA, born 13 November 1802, daughter of Reverend D. W., Rose and his wife Ann, died 25 August 1806. St Lucea gravestone, Jamaica]

ROSS, ALEXANDER, an American Loyalist, probably from South Carolina, who was granted land in St Elizabeth parish, Jamaica, in 1782. [TNA]

ROSS, DONALD, born 1749, a planter in Port Royal parish, died 18 September 1806. [Kingston gravestone, Jamaica]

ROSS, JOHN, a shipbuilder on Cape Fear, North Carolina, a Loyalist who moved to Kingston, Jamaica, in 1783. [TNA.AO12.36.327]

ROSS, JOHN, an American Loyalist, probably from South Carolina, who was granted land in St Elizabeth parish in 1782. [TNA]

ROSS, PETER, an American Loyalist, probably from South Carolina, who was granted land in St Elizabeth parish in 1782. [TNA]

ROUSE, JOSHUA, born 1765, from Jamaica, died in Southampton on 18 April 1842. [GM.ns17.574]

ROWE, Reverend GEORGE WILKINSON, in St Dorothy's, Jamaica, born 1808 son of Joshua Rowe in Devonport, died in Bideport, Devon, on 1 January 1867/ [GM.ns3/3.261]

ROWE, THOMAS, died in Jamaica, admin., 1657, PCC

ROWLAND, Miss, from Jamaica, married Major Fraser, ADC to Lieutenant General Nugent, in Liverpool on 13 April 1807. [GM.77.375]

ROWLEY, B. S., born 1764, Admiral of the Blue and Commander in Chief of HM fleet in Jamaica, died 7 October 1811. [Kingston gravestone, Jamaica]

ROWORTH, ..., son of C. E. W. Roworth of the 5th Regiment, was born in Newcastle, Jamaica, on 8 August 1865. [GM.ns2/19.635]

ROYKES, FRANCIS, born 1640, died 1709, husband of Elizabeth, parents of Francis born 1694, died 6 November 1708. [St John's gravestone, Jamaica]

RUDEN, ..., Captain, died in the earthquake of 1692. [JHR.viii.60-62]

RUGLESS, WILLIAM, born 1756, planter in St Andrew's, died 11 January 1796. [Spring Path, Kingston, gravestone, Jamaica]

RULE, JAMES, of Craggy Mount, St Thomas in the Vale, Jamaica, died in1797. [GM.67.986]

RUSSELL, DAPHNE, born 1684, died in Spanish Town, Jamaica, in 1801. [GM.71.376]

RUSSELL, H., of Caenwood Estate, St George's, Jamaica, died on passage from Bristol to Jamaica in 1813. [GM.83.670]

RUTHERFORD, or BURGER, ELIZABETH, born 1799, wife of W. J. Rutherford, died 8 October 1837. [Kingston gravestone, Jamaica]

RUTHERFORD, JAMES, died in Jamaica in 1791. [GM.61.682]

RUTHEFORD, WILLIAM, a planter in Jamaica, died 1754. [GM.24.579]

RYDE, ELIZABETH, born 1756, from Deptford, via London aboard the Nancy bound for Jamaica in 1774. [TNA.T47.9/11]

RYMES, HENRY, in Clarendon, Jamaica, probate, 1683, PCC

SACERDOTE, MOSES VITTA, probate, 1746, Jamaica. [BM.Add.ms21,931]

SADDLER, JAMES, born 1772 in London, on Weyhill Plantation, Jamaica, died in Jamaica on 26 August 1838. [GM.ns10.671]; Lucy, his widow, born 1791, died in Highgate on 8 October 1850. [GM.ns34.559]

SADDLER, RALPH, born 1759, a groom returning to Jamaica via London aboard the Amity Hall in 1774. [TNA.T47.9/11]

SALKEILD, THOMAS, died in Jamaica, admin., 1656, PCC

THE PEOPLE OF JAMAICA, 1655 TO 1855

SALMON, JOSEPH, sr., a merchant in Jamaica, 1670. [IRO.Deeds.iii.33]

SALMON, MARIA MULGRAVE, daughter of John Salmon the President of Jamaica, married George Wilson of the Royal Monmouth Light Infantry, in Elgin on 22 December 1859. [GM.ns2/8.179]

SALMON, THOMAS STOKES, died at Archibald Pen, St Elizabeth, Jamaica in 1793. [GM.63.1152]

SAMUDA, ALICE, daughter of Benjamin Samuda, from Jamaica, married Lyndon Howard Evelyn, the Customs Collector at Savanna la Mar, in Lund, Westmoreland, Jamaica, on 3 March 1821. [GM.91.467]

SAMUEL, DAVID, versus Jacob Israel Bernal, and others in Jamaica, an appeal to the Privy Council, 1787. [Bedford Record Office, OR1772]

SAMUELLS, PAUL STEVENS, from Jamaica, graduated MD from Edinburgh University in 1798. [EMG.29]

SANDERS, ABRAHAM, born 1762, a shipwright in Kingston, died 25 July 1815. [Spring Path, Kingston, gravestone, Jamaica]

SANDERS, HUMPHREY, fought at the Battle of Sedgemoor in Somerset, on 6 July 1685 against the forces of King James II, captured and transported from Portland Road aboard the Jamaican Merchant of London, master Charles Gardiner, bound for Jamaica in 1685.

SANDILANDS, JOHN, from East Barnet, died in Jamaica in April 1806. [GM.76.583]

SANFORD, BENJAMIN, MD, born 15 March 1798 in Connecticut, died on Windsor Estate, parish of St Ann, Jamaica, on 20 April 1832. [Windsor Estate gravestone, Jamaica]

SARE, GEORGE, a seaman aboard the <u>Sea Horse</u>, died in Jamaica, probate, 1692, PCC

SAUNDERS, JOHN, born 1736, a gentleman returning via Bristol to Jamaica aboard the <u>Charlotte Peg</u>in 1774. [TNA.T47.11]

SAUNDERSON, THOMAS, married Miss Lewis from London, in Jamaica in 1757. [GM.27.338]

SAVAGE, ARTHUR, born 1767, died on Strawberryhill Plantation, Port Royal, Jamaica, on 24 December 1814. [GM.85.278]

SAVELL, JOEL, in Jamaica, probate, 1787, PCC

SAXBY, MARK, died in Jamaica, administration, 1659, PCC

SAYER, EDWARD KYRWOOD, died in Jamaica on 24 March 1814. [GM.84.697]

SCARLETT, ELIZABETH, daughter of Philip Anglin Scarlett in Jamaica, died in Bristol on 14 November 1831. [GM.101.571]

SCARLETT, JAMES, married Miss Gallimore, daughter of Jarvis Gallimore, in Jamaica on 28 July 1791. [GM.61.774]

SCARLETT, ROBERT, from Jamaica, graduated MD from Edinburgh University in 1795. [EMG.26]

SCARLETT, Miss, daughter of James Scarlett, married Major General Riall, Governor of Grenada, in Jamaica in December 1819. [GM.89.635]-

SCARLETT, family, accounts of the Greenfield Plantation, Jamaica, 1789-1823. [Yorkshire Record Office, DDLA.41.1-14]

SCHAN, DANIEL, probate, 1735, Jamaica. [BM.Add.ms21,931]

SCHAW, Mrs, widow of Charles Schaw of Schawfield, Jamaica, married William Cruchley, from London, on 19 October 1795. [GM.65.878]

SCHURICH, JOHN JACOB, probate, 1731, Jamaica.
[BM.Add.ms21,931]

SCOTT, FRANCES, daughter of Reverend Scott in Port Royal, Jamaica, married Lieutenant Alexander Bucher of HMS Porcupine in 1793. [GM.63.860]

SCOTT, JAMES, in Kingston, Jamaica, died 1759. [GM.29.146]

SCOTT, J., Westminster and Jamaica, and F. M. Henderson, Putney and Jamaica, a marriage settlement, 1751. [BM.Add.ch.17265]

SCOTT, JOHN, a planter of 604 acres in St Andrew's parish in 1754. [TNA.CO137/28/171-196]

SCOTT, MATTHEW HENRY, born 1767 in Jamaica, a Vice Admiral, died in Southampton on 31 October 1836. [GM.ns7.321]

SCOTT, Mrs, born 1739, a lady, returning to Jamaica aboard the Dawes via Portsmouth in 1775. [TNA.T47.9/11]

SCRIVEN, THOMAS, from Henbury, Bristol, died at Buff Bay, Jamaica, on 29 August 1810. [GM.80.492]

SCROGIE, JOHN, born 1749, a planter, returning via London aboard the James Daukins for Jamaica in 1774. [TNA.T47.9/11]

SEALY, EDWARD, a mariner from London, died in Port Royal, Jamaica, probate, 1689, PCC

SEAMAN, MARY, daughter of W. B. Seaman in Vere, Jamaica, married Reverend James Saunders of Meek St Mary, Cornwall, in East Teignmouth, on 29 June 1853. [GM.ns40.305]

SEAMAN, W. G., born 1784, son of W. Seaman in Great Yarmouth, a surgeon in Vere, Jamaica, died in Spanish Town, Jamaica, on 15 January 1819. [GM.88.279]

SELLWOOD, WILLIAM, fought at the Battle of Sedgemoor in Somerset, on 6 July 1685 against the forces of King James II, captured and transported from Portland Road aboard the

THE PEOPLE OF JAMAICA, 1655 TO 1855

Jamaican Merchant of London, master Charles Gardiner, bound for Jamaica in 1685.

SELWYN, Brigadier WILLIAM, Governor of Jamaica, 1701.

SESSIONS, WILLIAM, died in Jamaica, admin., 1657, PCC

SEWELL, MARTIN, died in Jamaica in 1791. [GM.61.186]

SEWELL, ROBERT, born 1750, a barrister from London, with his wife born 1754, emigrating via Portsmouth aboard the Judith and Hilaria bound for Jamaica in 1776. [TNA.T47.9/11]

SHACKELFORD, HENRY, born 1733, from Jamaica, died in Peterfield, Hampshire, on 6 November 1821. [GM.91.478]

SHANNON, Mr, born 1786, a merchant in Kingston, Jamaica, was killed in 1811 on board the Pelican when it was attacked by the privateer Marengo. [GM.81.658]

SHARP, ANN, an indentured servant, from England to Port Royal, Jamaica, aboard the Saint George, Captain James, landed 3 January 1688, and sold for 45 dollars to Mr Moss, a merchant. [Taylor ms, Institute of Jamaica]

SHAW, CHARLES, born 1757, a planter returning to Jamaica via London aboard the Northampton in 1774. [TNA.T47.9/11]

SHAW, HENRY THOMAS, born 1823, son of Lee Shaw, and nephew of Sir Robert Shaw of Bushy Park, Dublin, died in Kingston, Jamaica, in June 1844. [GM.ns22.446]

SHAW, JOHN, in Jamaica, a letter, 1662. [Claredon ms76.146]

SHAW, JOHN HERCY, son of John Shaw in Jersey, died in Jamaica on 16 February 1843. [GM.ns20.110]

SHAW, Mrs, wife of Dr James Shaw, died in Kingston, Jamaica, on 22 February 1797. [GM.67.435]

SHEA, MATTHEW, died in Kingston, Jamaica, on 6 July 1803. [GM.73.882]

SHECKLES, JOHN, born 1712, settled in Jamaica in 1727, Custos Rotulorum of Cleveland and Vere, Brigadier General of Militia, died 17 June 1782. [Sheckles Estate, Claredon, gravestone, Jamaica]

SHEERES, ELLIOTT, from Stepney, London, died in Jamaica, administration, 1660, PCC

SHELLY, Miss, born 1796, daughter of Seba Shelly in St Anne's, Jamaica, niece of Mr Tippetts a surgeon in London, died in 1817. [GM.87.184]

SHELTON, FREDERICK RICHARD, son of Robert Shelton in Kennington, died on Serge Island Estate, Jamaica, on 3 November 1817. [GM.87.629]

SHERRARD, NOBLE, jr., from Bristol, died in Jamaica in 1818. [GM.88.90]

SHERWEN, Mrs DOUGLAS, wife of John Sherwen MD in Enfield, Middlesex, daughter of Dugald Campbell in Saltspring, Jamaica, died in Bath on 16 June 1804. [GM.74.601]

SHICKLE, ANN, widow of John Hayle Shickle, from Jamaica, died in Laugharne, Carmarthenshire, on 27 October 1840. [GM.ns14.675]

SHIFFNER, Mr, a merchant in Jamaica, died on 30 June 1762. [GM.32.448]

SHILLETO, W., born 1784, in Jamaica, died in London on 11 June 1838. [GM.ns10.224]

SHIRLAND, PETER, fought at the Battle of Sedgemoor in Somerset, on 6 July 1685 against the forces of King James II, captured and transported from Portland Road aboard the Jamaican Merchant of London, master Charles Gardiner, bound for Jamaica in 1685.

THE PEOPLE OF JAMAICA, 1655 TO 1855

SHIRLEY, HENRY, of Craycombe House, Worcestershire, died at Hyde Hall, Jamaica, in 1848. [GM.ns30.558]

SHIRLEY, Mrs, born 1759, widow of Edward Shirley of Petersfield, Jamaica, died in Clifton on 15 March 1808. [GM.78.167]

SHIRLING, GEORGE, died in Jamaica in 1790. [GM.60.1053]

SHOESMITH, ROBERT, fought at the Battle of Sedgemoor in Somerset, on 6 July 1685 against the forces of King James II, captured and transported from Portland Road aboard the Jamaican Merchant of London, master Charles Gardiner, bound for Jamaica in 1685.

SHORT, MAYOW, Chairman of the Quarter Sessions in Jamaica, married Rachel Annis Panton, daughter of Reverend Dr Panton in Widcombe, niece of the Vice Chancellor of Jamaica, on 15 June 1847. [GM.ns28.311]

SHURING, WILLIAM, born 1756, a gentleman from Bristol, to Jamaica via Bristol aboard the Hector in 1775. [TNA.T47.9/11]

SHUTE, WILLIAM, in Port Royal in 1682. [IRO.Deeds.xiv.10]

SILL, JOHN, a planter in Jamaica, died in Dent, Yorkshire, on 29 March 1803. [GM.73.386]

SILVESTER, ROBERT, from Chard, Somerset, died in Jamaica on 19 April 1841. [GM.ns16.222]

SIMBLET, JAMES, from Jamaica, died in Bath on 22 July 1757. [GM.27.386]

SIMMONIE, MARIE, born 1758, died 4 March 1828. [Spring Path, Kingston, gravestone, Jamaica]

SIMPSON, ELEANOR LAWRENCE, eldest daughter of John Simpson in Tiltston, Jamaica, married William Henry Bradley of the Bombay Medical Staff, in Bycullah on 16 November 1840. [GM.NS15.311]

THE PEOPLE OF JAMAICA, 1655 TO 1855

SIMPSON, Captain GEORGE, born 1801, son of Henry Simpson in Whitby, Yorkshire, master of the Palaniban of London, died in St Elizabeth's, Jamaica, on 10 June 1824. [GM.94.478]

SIMPSON, JOHN, an American Loyalist, probably from South Carolina, who was granted land in St Elizabeth parish, Jamaica, in 1782. [TNA]

SIMS, C. J., son of J.Sims in Walthamstow, Essex, an Assemblyman, died in Kingston, Jamaica, in 1813. [GM.83.595]; his widow, Frances, died in Walthamstow on 5 July 1816. [GM.86.93]

SIMS, FRANCES COCKBURN, daughter of C. J. Sims in Jamaica, married Viscount Valentia, son of the Earl of Mountnorris, in Brighton on 21 October1837. [GM.ns8.648]

SINCLAIR, DIANA, born 1753, from London, bound via London aboard the Fanny for Jamaica in 1774. [TNA.T47.9/11]

SINGER, ISAAC, in Jamaica, probate, 1802, PCC

SINGER, Mrs M. K., widow of George Singer in Jamaica, died in London in July 1809. [GM.79.785]

SINGLETON, FREDERIC, from Kingston, Jamaica, married Fanny Selfe, daughter of Samuel Selfe, in London on11 August 1853. [GM.ns40.521]

SLELEN, JOHN, died in Jamaica, administration, 1660, PCC

SKENE, ALEXANDER, an American Loyalist, probably from South Carolina, who was granted land in St Elizabeth parish, Jamaica, in 1782. [TNA]

SKENE, Dr JAMES, an American Loyalist, from South Carolina, who was granted land in St Elizabeth parish, Jamaica, in 1782; settled as a physician in S.C., moved to Kingston, Jamaica, by 1784. [TNA.AO12.52.163, etc]

THE PEOPLE OF JAMAICA, 1655 TO 1855

SKINNER, Mrs ELIZABETH, born 1773, widow of J. D. Skinner, from Jamaica, died in Little Ealing, Middlesex, on 28 December 1823. [GM.94.188]

SKURRAY, CHARLES THOMAS, born 1777, of St George's, Jamaica, died 1 October 1814. [GM.84.604]

SKUTT, THOMAS, a merchant in Jamaica, dead by 1673.

SLATER, JOHN, died in Kingston, Jamaica, in 1789. [GM.59.1209]

SLEATER, THOMAS, died in Jamaica in 1790. [GM.60.766]

SLOCOMBE, JEMIMA, daughter of Mr Slocombe of HM Customs in Jamaica, died in St Anne's, Jamaica, on 8 October 1810. [GM.81.85]

SMALLWOOD, WILLIAM, died in Jamaica, admin., 1657, PCC

SMART, JOHN, in Jamaica, probate, 1681, PCC

SMART, ROBERT, died in Kingston, Jamaica, on 5 June 1817. [GM.87.183]; his widow , daughter of John Willis in London, married James Cunningham in Jamaica on 17 November 1818. [GM.89.80]

SMITH, ADAM, and his wife Elizabeth, parents of Adam Smith, born 1799, died 1799, also Robert Smith, died 15 August 1799. [Sheckles Estate, Clarendon, gravestone, Jamaica]

SMITH, CHARLES, born 1747, a gardener from London, bound via London aboard the Charming Sally bound for Jamaica in 1774. [TNA.T47.9/11]

SMITH, CHARLES, born 1804, died in Kingston, Jamaica, on 11 Junr 1828. [Spring Path gravestone, Jamaica]

SMITH, Mrs ELIZABETH, born 1728, wife of Joseph Smith a carpenter in Kingston, died on 24 October 1768. [Kingston gravestone, Jamaica]

SMITH, E., from Eastley, Kent, in Kingston, Jamaica, was drowned off America in October 1834. [GM.105.222]

SMITH, FRANCIS, born 1740, a clergyman, returning to Jamaica via London aboard the Fanny in 1774. [TNA.T47.9/11]

SMITH, GEORGE, a dockyard clerk in Kingston, Jamaica, died on 20 October 1814. [GM.84.604]

SMITH, ISABELLA, wife of Colonel Smith of the Royal Artillery, died in Port Royal, Jamaica, in 1815. [GM.85.379]

SMITH, JAMES, and SAMUEL SMITH, in Jamaica, bonds, 1720. [Lincoln Archives. Ancaster 9.e.10]

SMITH, JAMES, born 1744, a gentleman returning to Jamaica via London aboard the William and Mary in 1774. [TNA.T47.9/11]

SMITH, JAMES, born 1742, died on Springhill Estate, Jamaica, on 24 February 1813. [GM.83.490]

SMITH, JOHN, fought at the Battle of Sedgemoor in Somerset, on 6 July 1685 against the forces of King James II, captured and transported from Portland Road aboard the Jamaican Merchant of London, master Charles Gardiner, bound for Jamaica in 1685.

SMITH, JOHN, born 1753, a gentleman and a merchant from London, bound via Liverpool aboard the St Peter for Jamaica in 1773. [TNA.T47.9/11]

SMITH, MATTHEW, from Aldburgh, Suffolk, died in Jamaica, admin., 1657, PCC

SMITH, NICHOLAS, died in Kingston, Jamaica, in 1799. [GM.69.719]

SMITH, RALPH, in Jamaica, 1683. [TNA. [Prob.4.22977]

SMITH, SAMUEL, born 1762, a husbandman from Somerlyton in Suffolk, bound aboard the Norfolk via Yarmouth for Jamaica in 1775. [TNA.T47.9/11]

SMITH, WILLIAM, in Jamaica, 1 May 1684. [TNA.Prob.4.18479]

SMITH, WILLIAM, a mariner from Bristol, died in Jamaica, probate, 1687, PCC

SMITH, WILLIAM, born 1748, an accountant, via Bristol aboard the Egale bound for Jamaica in 1775. [TNA.T47.9/11]

SMITH, WILLIAM TABOIS, married Eliza Gay Hannaford, daughter of Stephen Hannaford, in Jamaica on 7 April 1846. [GM.ns25.528]

SMITH, Dr, a resident of Jamaica for 50 years, died there on 11 July 1764. [GM.33.415]

SOAREZ, ARON JACOB, in Jamaica, petitioned the Council for Trade and Plantations in London, on 30 August 1692. [JCTP]

SOLEY, ELIZABETH, born 1760, from London, bound via London aboard the West Indian bound for Jamaica in 1774. [TNA.T47.9/11]

SOPER, JAMES, fought at the Battle of Sedgemoor in Somerset, on 6 July 1685 against the forces of King James II, captured and transported from Portland Road aboard the Jamaican Merchant of London, master Charles Gardiner, bound for Jamaica in 1685.

SPALDING, HELEN, daughter of Hinton Spalding MD, married William R. Myers, in Spanish Town, Jamaica, on 29 April 1845. [GM.ns24.189]

SPALDING, ROBERT, Surgeon General of the Surrey County Militia, died in Liguanea, Jamaica, on 17 June 1792. [GM.62.766]

SPARKE, CHARLES, in Barbados and Jamaica, 1638-1679, papers. [Royal Commonwealth Society, Sparke mss]

SPATH, PETER, born 1744, a sugar baker from London, bound via London aboard the London for Jamaica in 1773. [TNA.T47.9/11]

THE PEOPLE OF JAMAICA, 1655 TO 1855

SPEAR, RICHARD, born 1788, Secretary to Rear Admiral Douglas, died 14 November 1815. [St Andrew's gravestone, Jamaica] [GM.86.181]

SPENCE, GEORGE, from Jamaica, graduated MD at Edinburgh University in 1790. [EMG.22]

SPENCE, GEORGE, Chief Judge in Hanover, Jamaica, died in Lucea, Jamaica, on 30 September 1790. [GM.60.213]

SPENCE, JOHN, born 1754 in Yorkshire, late commander of the merchant ship Tabeth Vigilant, died 3 January 1785. [Maxfield Estate gravestone, Jamaica]

SPENCE, ROBERT, born 1751, a staymaker from London, via London aboard the Princess Carolina bound for Jamaica in 1774. [TNA.T47.9/11]

SPENCER, JOHN, died in Jamaica, admin., 1656, PCC

SPENCER, MARY SHAFTESBURY, daughter of Reverend Aubrey George Spencer the Bishop of Jamaica, wife of Reverend C. J. Smith the former Archdeacon of Jamaica, later in Erith, Kent, died in Hastings on 20 May 1854. [GM.ns42.91]

SPRAGG, Captain THOMAS, in Jamaica, a letter, 1688. [Salt Library, Stafford]

SPROULL, ANDREW, a merchant in Kingston, Jamaica, died on passage to Jamaica in 1802. [GM.72.785]

STANLEY, Lieutenant General THOMAS, brother of the Earl of Derby, died in Jamaica in 1779. [GM.50.50]

STANTON, Dr JAMES, died in Jamaica in 1790. [GM.60.1053]

STEELE, CHARLES JAMES, born 1827, son of James Steele in London, died in Ironshore Estate, Jamaica, on 7 August 1845. [GM.ns24.551]

STEELE, Miss, daughter of Reverend Dr Steele in Jamaica, marred Sir Thomas Ramsay of Balmain on 29 June 1809. [GM.79.676]

STENNETT, JOHN, from Jamaica, graduated MD from Edinburgh University in 1792. [EMG.23]

STEPHEN, WILLIAM, born 1772 in Aberdeen, died on passage from Jamaica on board the Orpheus on 7 July 1808. [GM.78.1039]

STEPHENS, CATHERINE, wife of Laurence Reade Stephens, died in Jamaica on 28 July 1818. [GM.88.469]

STEPHENS, THOMAS WILLIAM, born 1754, a clerk, died in St Jago de la Vega, Jamaica, on 6 September 1860. [GM.70.1107]

STEPHENSON, THOMAS, born 1744, a merchant from London, bound via London aboard the Susanna for Jamaica in 1774. [TNA.T47.9/11]

STEVENS, ISAAC, a merchant, died in Jamaica in 1791. [GM.61.1065]

STEVENSON, Reverend HENRY WILLIAM, born 1820, died in St Thomas in the Vale, Jamaica, on 10 January 1854. [GM.ns41.437]

STEVENSON, ISABELLA, daughter of William James Stevenson the Receiver General of Jamaica, married Henry John Kemble in St Andrew's, Jamaica, on 1 March 1851. [GM.ns35.545]

STEVENSON, JUSTICE, of the Supreme Court of Jamaica, married Caroline Octavia Biscoe, daughter of Joseph Seymour Biscoe of Pendhill, Surrey, in Barnwood on 9 June 1852. [GM.ns38.195]

STEVENSON, MARY CHARLOTTE, born 1813, wife of Justice Stevenson, died in Spanish Town, Jamaica, on 16 December 1850. [GM.ns35.334]

THE PEOPLE OF JAMAICA, 1655 TO 1855

STEVENSON, MARY LAURENCE, widow of William James Stevenson the Receiver General of Jamaica, died in Clifton on 27 December 1850. [GM.ns33.450]

STEVENSON, PETER, an American Loyalist, probably from South Carolina, who was granted land in St Elizabeth parish, Jamaica, in 1782. [TNA]

STEVENSON, ROBERT, a mariner from London, aboard the Constant Friend at Port Royal, Jamaica, probate, 1698, PCC

STEWART, CATHERINE, an American Loyalist, probably from South Carolina, who was granted land in St Elizabeth parish, Jamaica, in 1782. [TNA]

STEWART, CHARLES, from Llandovery, the Custos of St Ann's, Jamaica, died on 30 June 1854. [GM.ns42.314]

STEWART, MARY ANNE, eldest daughter of Walter George Stewart, Island Secretary, married Captain Barker, Royal Artillery, DC to the Governor, in Spanish Town, Jamaica, on 16 March 1852. [GM.ns37.612]

STEWART, MARY ELIZABETH, daughter of Reverend Thomas Stewart in Kingston, Jamaica, married Henry Westmoreland there on 30 April 1859. [GM.ns2/7.79]

STEWART, SARAH, daughter of Reverend S. H. Stewart in Trelawney, Jamaica, married Reverend T. Garrett of Vere, in Spanish Town, Jamaica, on 8 July 1854. [GM.ns42.385]

STEWART, SUSAN, wife of W. G. Stewart, the Island Secretary, died in Spanish Town, Jamaica, on 25 January 1856. [GM.ns45.434]

STEWART, WILLIAM, a gentleman, emigrated via Portsmouth aboard the Richmond bound for Jamaica in 1775. [TNA.T47.9/11]

STEWART, WILLIAM, son of William Stewart in Shambelly, died in Jamaica on 20 June 1799. [GM.69.812]

THE PEOPLE OF JAMAICA, 1655 TO 1855

STIRLING, WILLIAM, died in Jamaica in 1791. [GM.61.186]

STODY, ELIZABETH, daughter of John Stody in Jamaica, widow of Richard Highatt in Bristol, died on 23 March 1812. [GM.82.395]

STOGDON, JOHN, died at Martha Brae, Jamaica, on 19 October 1792. [GM.62.1220]

STOKES, EDWARD, a gentleman in Port Royal, Jamaica, probate, 1699, PCC

STOKES, Captain JAMES, died in Jamaica in 1791. [GM.61.1065]

STONEY, Reverend JOSEPH, in Trelawney, Jamaica, died in July 1789. [GM.59.955]

STOPFORD, THOMAS, a Captain of the Royal Navy, died 10 October 1824. [Kingston gravestone, Jamaica]

STORER, CHARLOTTE, daughter of Anthony Gilbert Storer in Berkshire, died in Jamaica on 7 July 1831. [GM.101.286]

STORER THOMAS, died at Golden Square, Westmoreland, Jamaica, on 11 July 1793. [GM.63.1149]

STORER, Miss, daughter of Thomas Storer in Golden Square, Jamaica, married John Campbell, in Jamaica on 10 March 1774. [GM.44.141]

STORMONTH, JAMES, a surgeon, died in St Mary's, Jamaica, on 1 October 1801. [GM.71.1211]

STOTT, WILLIAM, sr., a merchant planter in Kingston and Port Royal, Jamaica, died 1 November 1809. [GM.79.1175]

STOTT, Mrs, a widow, died in Jamaica in January 1784. [GM.54.395]

STRACHAN, ARCHIBALD, born 1782, died in Manchioneal, Jamaica, on 13 November 1828. [GM.99.190]

THE PEOPLE OF JAMAICA, 1655 TO 1855

STRATON, THOMAS, a planter of 8 acres in St Andrew's parish, Jamaica, in 1754. [TNA.CO137/28/171-196]

STREET, JEREMY, from Jamaica, died in London on 21 September 1781. [GM.51.443]

STRUPAR, FRANCES MASSEY, born 1788, died 30 December 1824. [Belle Vue gravestone, Jamaica]

STUART, ROBERT, born 1770, son of John Stuart in Birkenburn, Banffshire, from Port Morant, Jamaica, died in Hazely Heath, Hampshire, on 29 June 1813. [GM.83.666]

STYLES, JOHN, settled in St John's, Jamaica, in 1665, as a planter. [CSP.1669-1674.270]

SULTAN, JOHN, son of John Sultan, died 23 August 1745. [Chapleton gravestone, Claredon, Jamaica]

SUSANNAH, an indentured servant, from England to Port Royal, Jamaica, aboard the Saint George, Captain James, landed 3 January 1688, and sold for 40 dollars to Mr Colson, the Withywood vintner. [Taylor ms, Institute of Jamaica]

SUTHERLAND, GRACE, daughter of William Sutherland in Jamaica, married R. T. Lyney from London, on 23 December 1819. [GM.89.635]

SUTTON, Colonel THOMAS, born 1638, died 15 November 1710. [Vere gravestone, Jamaica]

SWABY, ANN MARGARET ELEANOR, daughter of Joseph James Swaby in Kilnsey, Yorkshire, grand-daughter of Joseph James Swaby, from Jamaica, married Frederick Peat, in Jamaica on 5 March 1842. [GM.ns.17.661]

SWABY, GEORGE, of Jamaica, graduated MD from Edinburgh University in 1822. [EMG]

THE PEOPLE OF JAMAICA, 1655 TO 1855

SWAINE, HARRY, born 1818, son of T. Swaine MD in Rochford, Essex, died in Jamaica in 1840. [GM.ns13.559]

SWARTON, WILLIAM, in Jamaica, died on 30 June 1762. [GM.32.448]

SWIMMER, ANTHONY, from Bristol, late of Jamaica, probate, 1688, PCC; [IRO.Deeds.v.96]

SWYMMER, ANTHONY, died 23 January 1729. [Morant Bay gravestone, Jamaica]

SWYMMER, ANTHONY LANGLEY, died in Jamaica in 1760. [GM.30.154]

SWINEY, MATTHEW, a Customs Collector, died in Savanna la Mar, Jamaica, on 24 December 1792. [GM.62.279]

SWINTON, JOHN, a mariner in Port Royal, Jamaica, probate, 1697, PCC

SYAR, WILLIAM, died in Jamaica, admin., 1657, PCC

SYLVESTER, JAMES, in Jamaica, died in October 1757. [GM.27.577]

SYMES, WILLIAM LEIGH, of Offord Hall, Northamptonshire, died on Oxford Estate, St Mary's, Jamaica, on 20 December 1796. [GM.67.350]

SYMPSON, Dr ARCHIBALD, an Assemblyman, died in Jamaica in 1791. [GM.61.1065]

SYMPSON, EDWARD, born 1812, formerly in the Royal Navy, died in Monymusk, Jamaica, in 1846. [GM.ns25.670]

SYMPSON, GEORGE, died in Jamaica, admin, 1657, PCC

TAAFFE, Dr., died in Jamaica in 1791. [GM.61.971]

TALBOTT, CHARLES, from Westminster, died in Jamaica, probate, 1688, PCC

THE PEOPLE OF JAMAICA, 1655 TO 1855

TALBOTT, EDWARD, from Southwold, Suffolk, died on the <u>Great Charity</u> at Jamaica, admin., 1656, PCC

TALBOTT, JOHN, from Yarmouth, Norfolk, died in Jamaica, admin., 1656, PCC

TAPSCOTT, WILLIAM, fought at the Battle of Sedgemoor in Somerset, on 6 July 1685 against the forces of King James II, captured and transported from Portland Road aboard the <u>Jamaican Merchant of London</u>, master Charles Gardiner, bound for Jamaica in 1685.

TATHAM, WILLIAM, son of John Tatham in London, died in Kingston, Jamaica, on 18 February 1794. [GM.64.384]

TAVENS, D., born 1760, a gentleman returning to Jamaica via London aboard the <u>New Shoreham</u> in 1774. [TNA.T47.9/11]

TAVERES, ABRAHAM, jr., late of Jamaica, dead by 1798, an indenture. [Car.3.25]

TAVAREZ, DAVID, probate, 1746, Jamaica. [BM.Add.ms 21,931]

TAWS, JOHN, a planter, died on Lady Mayo's estate in St John's, Jamaica, in 1800. [GM.70.905]

TAYLOR, ELIZA, daughter of John Taylor, Good Hope, Jamaica, married William Grove Annesley, Captain of the 6th Regiment, son of General A. G. Annesley of County Cork, in St Michael's in the Port Royal Mountains, Jamaica, on 8 March 1866. [GM.ns3/1.737]

TAYLOR, G. L., married Sybilla Neufville, daughter of Jacob Neufville, in Jamaica on 8 June 1820. [GM.90.635]

TAYLOR, GEORGE, born 1812, nephew of Arthur Foulkes in Jamaica, died there on 25 October 1833. [GM.104.118]

TAYLOR, JOHN, master of the <u>Bonadventure</u> trading between Port Royal, Gambia, and Bristol in 1691. [TNA.CO145/13.217-220]

THE PEOPLE OF JAMAICA, 1655 TO 1855

TAYLOR, Sir JOHN, died in Kingston, Jamaica, on 6 May 1786. [GM.56.619]

TAYLOR, SIMON, in Kingston, Jamaica, re Rigby Estate in Jamaica, 1791-1792. [Essex Record Office, D/DHw.A73A]

TAYLOR, SIMON, born 1740, an Assemblyman, died in Port Royal, Jamaica, on 14 April 1813. [GM.83.1813]

TAYLOR, THOMAS, a tavern keeper in Port Royal in 1674. [Jamaica Archives, inventory, liber i]

TAYLOR, Mr, born 1753, a gentleman, to be store-keeper in HM Dockyard in Jamaica, via Portsmouth aboard the Ipswich bound for Jamaica in 1775. [TNA.T47.9/11]

TAYLOR, Mrs, wife of John Taylor in Jamaica, died in London in 1803. [GM.73.89]

TELFAIR, Mrs ELIZABETH, an American Loyalist, probably from South Carolina, who was granted land in St Elizabeth parish, Jamaica, in 1782. [TNA]

TELFAIR, WILLIAM, an American Loyalist, probably from South Carolina, who was granted land in St Elizabeth parish, Jamaica, in 1782. [TNA]

TELFER, JAMES, son of Patrick and Anne Telfer, died 1788. [Falmouth gravestone, Jamaica]

TELFER, Mr, from Trelawney, Jamaica, died in London on 30 October 1812. [GM.82.498]

TERNAUX, LOUIS, in Kingston, Jamaica, a letter, 1809. [Yorkshire Record Office.DDHO.13.27]

TERRELL, KOSIUSKO, son of William and Mary Terrell in Bristol, died 1821. Falmouth gravestone, Jamaica]

THE PEOPLE OF JAMAICA, 1655 TO 1855

TERRITT, SARAH, born 1757, wife of Dr Territt, and sister of Crawford Ricketts, in Kingston, Jamaica, died on 21 September 1802. [GM.72.886]

TERRY, NATHANIEL, in Kingston, Jamaica, probate, 16 October 1695, PCC; [TNA.Prob.11427.349]

THARP, BENJAMIN H., in Hampton, Jamaica, died on 24 July 1851. [GM.ns36.442]

THARP, GRACE, daughter of Captain John Tharpe, a mariner, and his wife Margaret, died in 1796. [Falmouth gravestone, Jamaica]

THARP, JOHN, of Greenpond, born 1752, died 1811. [Montego Bay gravestone, Jamaica]

THARP, THOMAS REID, son of Benjamin H. Tharp, died in Jamaica on 3 September 1851. [GM.ns36.553]

THARP, WILLIAM, Lieutenant Colonel of the St James Militia Regiment, died on Windsor Castle Estate, Montego Bay, Jamaica, on 2 March 1809. [GM.79.677]

THISTLEWOOD, JOHN, {?} in Jamaica, 1764-1765. [Lincolnshire Archives. Monson. 31.90]

THISTLEWOOD, THOMAS, a planter in Westmoreland, Jamaica, journals, 1748 – 1786, [Lincoln Archives. Monson. 31/1-37]; on Bread Nutt Island, Jamaica, meteorological journals, 1770-1776. [BM. Add. 18275A-B]

THOM, JOHN, a land surveyor, brother of Robert Thom HM Consul at Ningpo, died in Clarendon, Jamaica, on 18 May 1851. [GM.ns36.100]

THOMAS, JOHN, born 1749, a merchant, via Newcastle aboard the Experiment bound for Jamaica in 1775. [TNA.T47.9/11]

THE PEOPLE OF JAMAICA, 1655 TO 1855

THOMSON, ALEXANDER, an American Loyalist, probably from South Carolina, who was granted land in St Elizabeth parish, Jamaica, in 1782. [TNA]

THOMPSON, ARCHIBALD, a merchant, did in Liguenea, Jamaica, on 11 November 1792. [GM.62.1220]

THOMSON, JANE, daughter of Archibald Thomson in Jamaica, married Henry Bowyer a Major of the Royal Artillery, in Greenham, Berkshire, on 2 February 1825. [GM.95.177]

THOMPSON, JOHN, born 1741, a merchant from Liverpool, bound aboard the Mary via Liverpool to Jamaica in 1774. [TNA.T47.9/11]

THOMSON, JOHN, born 1757, a clerk from London, bound via London aboard the Catherine for Jamaica in 1774. [TNA.T47.9/11]

THOMSON, ROBERT, from Jamaica, married Jane Kennedy, daughter of Robert Kennedy of Daljarrock, in Maybole, Ayrshire, on 4 January 1796. [GM.66.80]

THOMSON, ROBERT, of Lorn, born 1756, died in Kingston, Jamaica, on 14 October 1801. [Kingston gravestone, Jamaica]

THOMPSON, WILLIAM, in Jamaica, died 4 November 1767. [GM.37.563]

THORNBURY, C., born 1787, son of Reverend W. Thornbury in Avening, Gloucestershire, died in Port Royal, Jamaica, in 1813. [GM.83.595]

THORNTON, ROBERT, a staff surgeon, married Mary Robson, daughter of William Wealands Robson of Bishopwearmouth, in Kingston, Jamaica, on 24 March 1860. [GM.ns2/8.507]

THORPE, JOHN, from Chippenham Hall, Cambridge, a merchant, died in Jamaica in 1804. [GM.74.1175]

TICHBONE, THOMAS, from Jamaica, married Miss Jones in Mitcham, Surrey, in 1758. [GM.78.94]

THE PEOPLE OF JAMAICA, 1655 TO 1855

TICKELL, PATRICK, a mariner from Stepney, London, died in Jamaica, probate, 1680, PCC

TIERNEY, JAMES, died in Kingston, Jamaica, on 18 July 1784. [GM53.797]

TOBOIS, DAVID, born 1842, died 5 August 1869. [St John's gravestone, Jamaica]

TOCKLOVE, THOMAS, a mariner from Wapping, London, died aboard the ship John and Sarah at Jamaica, probate, 1693, PCC

TODD, ELIZA, daughter of Utten J. Todd in The Ridge, Jamaica, married Henry John Blagrove, in London on 25 July 1850. [GM.ns34.540]

TOMKINS, PHILIP, in Jamaica, died in 1753. [GM.23 591]

TOMPION, ROBERT SWETE, married Elizabeth Porter from London, in Jamaica in April 1752. [GM.22.240]

TONGE, WINKSWORTH, Deputy Judge Advocate of the Forces in Jamaica, died 12 July 1820. [St John's gravestone, Jamaica]

TORRES, DAVID LOPES, a merchant in Jamaica, executor of Isaac Larnego, [Car.3,155]; probate, 1816, PCC

TORRES, JACOB TORRES, overseer of the synagogue in Port Royal in 1686. [Journal of the House of Assembly in Jamaica. i.114]

TORRES, JACOB LOPEZ, probate, 12 April 1768

TORRES, LOPEZ SARAH, probate, 1735, Jamaica. [BM.Add.ms 21,931]

TORRES, ..., born 1687, a Jewess, died in Spanish Town, Jamaica, in 1799. [GM.69.624]

TORY, NETLAM, born 1783, from Jamaica, died in Everton on 18 February 1855. [GM.ns43.444]

TRAIL, Dr DAVID, died in Jamaica in 1791. [GM.61.187]

THE PEOPLE OF JAMAICA, 1655 TO 1855

TRELAWNEY, Colonel EDWARD, Governor of Jamaica, petition, 1745. [BM.West. Add.34736, f.145]

TREW, ANN, born in 1800, wife of John M. Trew, died 29 March 1842. [Kingston gravestone, Jamaica]

TOTTERDALE, HUGH, a lawyer in Jamaica, was proposed for the Council of Jamaica, 1711. [Salt Library, Stafford]

TRAVERS, HORACE, Assistant Commissary General, died in Jamaica on 25 June 1867. [GM.ns3/2.397]

TRAVERS, JOHN TAYLOR, son of Joseph Travers, died in Jamaica on 23 July 1845. [GM.ns24.438]

TRELAWNEY, EDWARD, son of Sir James Trelawney in Winchester, Governor of Jamaica, married Miss Crawford the niece of the Countess of Dartmouth, on 8 November 1737. [GM.7.701]; he died in Jamaica on 16 January 1754, [GM.12.107]; she died in January 1742. [GM.12.107]

TRELAWNEY, Colonel Sir William Trelawney, Governor of Jamaica, died in 1773, [GM.43.103]; his widow died on 13 May 1782. [GM.52.263]

TRICKETT, MATTHEW, and his wife Mary, from the Isle of Wight, died in Kingston, Jamaica, in August 1853. [GM.ns40.429]

TRIPE, ALGERNON, born 1820, son of C. Tripe in Devonport, a clerk in the Ordnance Department in Jamaica, died on Ordnance Island on 8 June 1850. [GM.ns34.230]

TROUP, Miss, in Jamaica, married Henry Darlot of the Foreign Post Office, on 6 March 1800. [GM.70.282]

TRUPE, GEORGE, born 1755, a carpenter from London, bound via London aboard the Royal Charlotte for Jamaica in 1774. [TNA.T47.9/11]

THE PEOPLE OF JAMAICA, 1655 TO 1855

TRUSCOTT, Dr, born 1780, son of Admiral Truscott in Exeter, died in Jamaica in 1813. [GM.83.183]

TUCKER, RICHARD, from the Isle of Wight, died in Jamaica, admin., 1657, PCC

TULLOCH, ALEXANDER FRANCIS TANNACHIE, son of Francis Tulloch formerly Major of the Inverness Militia, died in Jamaica on 23 March 1835. [GM.ns4.102]

TULLY, ADELAIDE ELIZABETH, daughter of James Dillon Tully, MD, Inspector General of Hospitals in Jamaica, married Edward Graham, son of Sir Robert Graham of Esk, Cumberland, in London on 3 August 1844. [GM.ns22.422]

TULLY, Dr, a Hospital Inspector, died in Jamaica on 3 September 1827. [GM.97.477]

TURNBULL, DAVID, a judge, married Alice Marshall, daughter of John Marshall of Paynter Vale in Bermuda, in Jamaica on 1 August 1844. [GM.ns22.538]

TURNER, CAROLINE, daughter of D. S. Turner in Clarendon, Jamaica, married J. F. Smith, a Writer to the Signet in Edinburgh, in London on 12 June 1830. [GM.100.554]

TURNER, SARAH, wife of Reverend Thomas Bryett Turner in Port Royal, Jamaica, died inKingston, Jamaica, on20 July 1856. [GM.ns2/1.519]

TWISTLETON, WILLIAM, a mariner from London, died in Jamaica, probate, 1685, PCC

TWITTEE, ROBERT, died in Jamaica, admin., 1657, PCC

TYRRELL, JAMES, in Portland, Jamaica, married Anne Codrington, daughter of John Codrington in Machineal, Jamaica, on 23 June 1792. [GM.62.1151]

THE PEOPLE OF JAMAICA, 1655 TO 1855

USHER, TOWNSEND, from Bristol, died in Kingston, Jamaca, in November 1810. [GM.81.34]

UTTEN, HARRIOT, widow of James P. Utten, daughter of Duncan Campbell, in Jamaica, died in Brompton on 11 November 1845. [GM.ns24.658]; James died in Jamaica on 15 November 1841. [GM.ns17.231]

VALENTINE, JOHN, born 1751, a watchmaker from Derby, bound via London aboard the William and Mary for Jamaica in 1774. [TNA.T47.9/11]

VALLETTE, PETER, in Jamaica, died in 1762. [GM.32.45]

VAN BEELEN, JOHN, died in St Elizabeth's, Jamaica, on 15 August 1793. [GM.63.1051]

VASSALL, RICHARD, born 1732 in Jamaica, died in London on 28 February 1795. [GM.65.349]

VAUGHAN, BENJAMIN, married Sarah Manning, daughter of William Manning of St Mary Axe, in Jamaica on 30 June 1781. [GM.51.342]

VAUGHAN, JAMES, in 96 District, S.C., a Loyalist soldier, settled in St James parish, Jamaica, in 1783. [TNA.AO13.123.318-377]

VAUGHAN, JOHN, born 1715, a grocer from Shrewsbury, via London aboard the Nancy bound for Jamaica in 1774. [TNA.T47.9/11]

VAUGHAN, SAMUEL, Chief Clerk of the Supreme Court of Jamaica, 1736-1752. [Northampton, Grafton MS.1978-90]

VAUGHAN, SAMUEL, '58 years in Jamaica', Assemblyman for St James, judge of Cornwall, died on Ridgeland Estate, Jamaica, on 9 February 1827. [GM.96.478]

VAUGHAN, W. WELBY, son of Mr Vaughan in Leicester, died in Spanish Town, Jamaica, in 1803. [GM.73.1254]

THE PEOPLE OF JAMAICA, 1655 TO 1855

VERDUGO, AARON, probate, 1745, Jamaica. [BM.Add.ms 21,931]

VERMONT, THOMAS ROBERT, born 1802, from Hayes, Middlesex, a magistrate in Trelawney, Jamaica, died in Falmouth, Jamaica, on 6 September1864. [GM.ns2/18.114]

VERNON, Admiral Sir Edward, in Jamaica, 1741. [NLS.ms.591/1889]

VERNON, JAMES, a planter in St James's parish, Jamaica, 1783, an affidavit. [see TNA.AO.128.2.18-263]

VERNON, JAMES, from Jamaica, graduated MD from Edinburgh University in 1796. [EMG.26]

VICAR, EDWARD, in St Lucia's, Jamaica, a letter of attorney, 1751. [Sheffield Central Library.MD170]

VIDAL, ELIZA, wife of Dr William Henry Vidal, and niece of Jesse Foot in Ilfracombe, Devon, died in St Mary's, Jamaica, on 21 November 1825. [GM.96.94]

VIDAL, JOHN JAMES, the Assemblyman for St Thomas in the Vale, Jamaica, and a judge, died in Clifton on 22 October 1823. [GM.93.572]

VILLETTES, General WILLIAM A., Lieutenant Governor of Jamaica, died in Port Antonio, Jamaica, on 3 July 1808. [GM.78.852]

VIRGIN, SAMUEL, born 1737, from Jamaica, died in London on 22 February 1815. [GM.85.280]

VIRGO, JAMES, died in Jamaica in 1791. [GM.61.186]

VRIGNEAUX, JEAN, born 1765 in Rochfort, France, died 20 September 1835. [Spring Path gravestone, Kingston, Jamaica]

WAAG, MOSES, probate, 1745, Jamaica. [BM.Add.ms 21,931]

WAGSTAFFE, John, husband of Mary Wagstaffe, she was born 1723, died 7 December 1760], parents of Peter Wagstaffe born 1742, died 16 December 1759. [Kingston gravestone, Jamaica]

THE PEOPLE OF JAMAICA, 1655 TO 1855

WALE, JAMES, postmaster of Jamaica, 1687. [IRO]

WALKER, CATHERINE, daughter of Dr Walker, Physician General of Jamaica, and wife of Thomas Deane, a merchant in Kingston, Jamaica, died in St John's, Jamaica, in 1826. [GM.96.191]

WALKER, HENRY, born 1805, from Jamaica, died in Northumberland in 1827. [GM.97.188]

WALKER, Sir HOVEDEN, in Jamaica, journal, 1719. [HMC.3]

WALKER, JOHN, born 1729, '35 years in Jamaica', proprietor og *The Jamaica Gazette*, died in Kingston, Jamaica, on 20 June 1786. [GM.56.810]

WALKER, TIMOTHY, a gentleman, emigrated via Portsmouth aboard the Richmond bound for Jamaica in 1775. [TNA.T47.9/11]

WALLACE, JAMES, an American Loyalist, probably from South Carolina, who was granted land in St Elizabeth parish, Jamaica, in 1782. [TNA]

WALLER, THOMAS, born 1754, a merchant from London, from London aboard the Lady's Adventure bound for Jamaica in 1776. [TNA.T47.9/11]

WALLIS, ..., son of William Beale Wallis a surgeon, was born in Kingston, Jamaica, on 7 June 1864. [GM.ns2/17.2311]

WALTERS, WILLIAM, born 1757, a gentleman from Andover, bound via Bristol aboard the Hector for Jamaica in 1775. [TNS.T47.9/11]

WALTON, Dr RICHARD, in Jamaica, a petition to the Privy Council, Colonial, 2 June 1709. [APCCol.223]

WARD, Reverend VALENTINE, the General Superintendent of the Weslayan Mission in the West Indies, died in Jamaica on 26 March 1835. [GM.ns4.102]

THE PEOPLE OF JAMAICA, 1655 TO 1855

WARD, Dr W., a physician from Bristol, died in Kingston, Jamaica, in 1811. [GM.81.656]

WARDEN, Mrs SARAH, born 1773, wife of W. R. Warden, died 29 August 1811. [Kingston gravestone, Jamaica]

WARE, ROBERT, born 1759, a bookkeeper from London, bound via London aboard the Capel for Jamaica in 1774. [TNA.T47.9/11]

WARGE, THOMAS, born 1747, a planter from Berwick on Tweed, bound via London aboard the Jamaica for Jamaica in 1774. [TNA.T47.9/11]

WARNER, HENRY, a barrister, son of Ashton Warner the Chief Justice of Trinidad, died in Jamaica on 25 July 1843. [GM.ns29.445]

WARREN, EDWARD B., a magistrate in Port Royal, Jamaica, brother of Thomas Warren a wholesale druggist in Bristol, died in Jamaica on 27 June 1836. [GM.ns6.668]

WARREN, THOMAS FULLERTON, born 1780, from Jamaica, died in Brompton, Middlesex, on 39 December 1813. [GM.84.97]

WASS, ERICH, a surgeon from Aldgate, London, died in Jamaica, probate, 1692, PCC

WATELY, ROBERT, born 1730, a merchant in Kingston, Jamaica, died 26 October 1755.

WATERHOUSE, JOHN, born 1769, son of Benjamin Waterhouse in Jamaica died on 27 March 1854. [GM.41.557]

WATERHOUSE, JULIA, daughter of John Waterhouse in Kingston, Jamaica, married Thomas Benton of Thorp Arch, Yorkshire, in Brenchley, Kent, on 9 July 1862. [GM.ns2/13.225]

WATERHOUSE, SUSANNAH, widow of Benjamin Waterhouse in Jamaica, died in London on 20 March 1809. [GM.79.386]

THE PEOPLE OF JAMAICA, 1655 TO 1855

WATERHOUSE, SUSAN, daughter of Benjamin Waterhouse in Kingston, Jamaica, married R. W. Carpenter in Bath on 3 April 1846. [GM.ns25.639]

WATERLAND, I., in Jamaica, died 7 December 1757. [GM.27.577]

WATKINS, MOSES, a carpenter and owner of 'The Cat and Fiddle' in Port Royal, Jamaica, 1689, [IRO.Deeds. xxi.84]; probate, 1691. [TNA.Prob.20.2902]

WATKINS, PRICE, born 1802, a barrister, from Greenwich Park, Jamaica, died in Shrewsbury in March 1836. [GM.ns5.675]

WATSON, ELIZABETH, born 1758, daughter of John Watson in St Elizabeth's, Jamaica, died in London on 10 April 1800. [GM.70.390]

WATSON, Sir FRANCIS, of St Martin-in-the-Feld, London, died in Jamaica, probate, 1692, PCC

WATSON, JAMES, in Jamaica, died 1763. [GM.33.518]

WATSON, JOHN, born 1769, from Trelawney, Jamaica, died in Fortrose on 5 December 1810. [GM.81.492]

WATSON, THOMAS, a merchant in Port Royal, 1683. [IRO.Deeds.xiii.187]

WATT, ANN, daughter of Robert Watt in Jamaica, married James Anderson from Edinburgh, at Stratford Bow on 30 December 1840. [GM.ns15.199]

WATTS, GEORGE, a gentleman, late at Jamaica, probate, 1656, PCC

WATTS, NATHANIEL, a grocer in Bristol and in Jamaica, probate, 1692, PCC

WEBB, JOHN, from Jamaica, died in London in 1779. [GM.45.46]

WEBB, THOMAS, born 1798, died in Jamaica on 30 July1845. [GM.ns24.438]

WEBB, WILLIAM, a soldier at Jamaica, probate, 1656, PCCA

WEBLEY, EDWARD, an Assemblyman and Chief Justice of Jamaica, died in 1777. [GM.ns47.555]

WEBSTER, NATHANIEL, born 1754, a gentleman from London, bound via London aboard the Henry for Jamaica in 1774. [TNA.T47.9/11]

WEDDERBURN, JAMES, an attorney and proprietor in Jamaica, died in July 1797. [GM.62.889]

WEDDERSPOON, LAURENCE, born 1701, died 25 April 1787. [Tennants' gravestone, Clarendon, Jamaica]

WEIR, JAMES, a merchant in Charleston from 1771, moved to Jamaica in 1782, who was granted land in St Elizabeth parish, Jamaica, in 1782. [TNA.AO12.51.249, etc]

WELCH, GEORGE, a merchant in Port Royal, Jamaica, dead by 1671, son of William Welch a merchant in London. [IRO.Deeds.v.26]

WELLERY, JOHN, born 1754, a gentleman returning to Jamaica via London aboard the New Shoreham in 1774. [TNA.T47.9/11]

WELLS, JOHN, a merchant in Port Royal, Jamaica, 1683, [IRO.Deeds.xiii.187]; probate, 1684, PCC

WELMORE, CATHERINE, born 1746, a servant from London, bound via London aboard the St James to Jamaica in 1775. [TNA.T47.9/11]

WEMYSS, ALEXANDER, died in Jamaica in 1791. [GM.61.1065]

WESCOMB, RICHARD, in Port Royal, Jamaica, probate, 1696, PCC

WEST, SARAH, daughter of William Henry West in Jamaica, married John Campbell from Colesberg at the Cape of Good Hope, in London on 1 November 1842. [GM.ns19.86]

WEST, WILLIAM, born 1798, son of John West of Jamaica and of Surrey, died in Portland, Jamaica, on 27 November 1833. [GM.104.343]

WESTBROOKE, CALEB, a goldsmith in Jamaica, probate, 1693, PCC

WESTMACOTT, RICHARD, married Miss D. Wilkinson, in Jamaica on 30 February 1798. [GM.68.255]

WESTMORELAND, HENRY, married Elizabeth Stewart, daughter of Reverend Thomas Stewart, in Kingston, Jamaica, on 30 April 1859. [GM.ns2/7.79]

WESTMORELAND, HERBERT, born 1828, son of Isaac Westmorland in London, and brother of Henry Westmorland, died at Etingdon Estate, Trelawney, on 10 March 1846. [Annotto Bay gravestone, Jamaica]

WESTON, WILLIAM, born 1753, a gentleman from London, bound via London aboard the Ashley for Jamaica in 1774. [TNA.T47.9/11]

WHALLEY, CHARLES, a gentleman from London, died in Jamaica, probate, 1690, PCC

WHYTE, ELIZABETH GOULD, daughter of David Whyte in Jamaica, died in Brighton on 23 August 1808. [GM.78.855]

WHITE, FREDERICK, a magistrate in Jamaica, diary, 1834-1835. [Rhodes House Library, Oxford]

WHITE, JAMES CLAYTON, Custos of Portland, Major of Militia, died in Jamaica on 13 July 1834. [GM.104.558]

WHITE, Mrs MARY, died in Kingston, Jamaica, in 1793. [GM.63.1152]

WHITE, THOMAS, in Jamaica in 1674. [IRO.Deeds.i.245]

WHITE, T., son of Mrs White in Grantham, Lincolnshire, died in Spanish Town, Jamaica, on 24 May 1794. [GM.64.671]

THE PEOPLE OF JAMAICA, 1655 TO 1855

WHITE, WILLIAM, a planter in Jamaica, 1819-1826. [Essex Record Office.D.DCe.F11]

WHITE, Mr, born 1738, a planter, returning via London aboard the James Daukins for Jamaica in 1774. [TNA.T47.9/11]

WHITEFOORD, Reverend CALEB, born 1842, son of Reverend C. Whitefoord in Whitton, Shropshire, died in Fullerswood, Jamaica, on 5 August 1866. [GM.ns3/2.551]

WHITEHORNE, JAMES RISBY, a judge, died in St Anne's, Jamaica, in 1789. [GM.59.573]

WHITEHORNE, SAMUEL, a judge in St Catherine's, and a barrister, died in Carravina, Jamaica, in December 1796. [GM.67.350]

WHITEHORNE, WILLIAM FREDERICK, died in Chiswick, St Thomas in the East, Jamaica, on 8 September 1846. [GM.ns26.559]

WHITELEY, FREDERICK, a surgeon, son of Reverend Joseph Whiteley in Leeds, died in Jamaica on 16 December 1832. [GM.102.382]

WHITELOCK, H. N., in Hanover county, Jamaica, a letter, 1848. [BM. Peel ms. Add.40600. ff43-8]

WHITFIELD, Lieutenant Colonel CHARLES, a merchant in Jamaica, 1669. [IRO.Deeds.i.105]

WHITLOCK, WILLIAM, a planter returning via Portsmouth to Jamaica aboard the Thetis in 1776. [TNA.T47.9/11]

WHITESIDE, THOMAS, died 1850. [Falmouth gravestone, Jamaica]

WHITTLE, CHARLES, a merchant in Port Royal, Jamaica, probate, 1697, PCC

WICKHAM, WILLIAM, died in Jamaica, admin., 1657, PCC

WIGGLESWORTH, Mr, formerly the Commissary General in St Domingo, died in Jamaica on 21 March 1800. [GM.70.486]

THE PEOPLE OF JAMAICA, 1655 TO 1855

WIGNALL, ELEAZER, gentleman in Morant parish, Jamaica, 1683. [IRO.Deeds.xvii.70]

WILCKENS, JACOB FREDERICK, born 1757, died in Kingston, Jamaica, on 12 June 1826. [GM.96.574]

WILDBORE, JOHN, a citizen and mercer of London, died in Port Royal, Jamaica, probate, 1688, PCC

WILKIE, ROBERT BALL, born 1817, son of Major Wilkie in Bristol, died in Hanover, Jamaica, on 13 January 1850. [GM.ns33.343]

WILKINSON, JAMES, in Jamaica, died on 2 June 1779. [GM.ns38.411]

WILLIAMS, ALICE PIERCE, wife of Bartholomew Owen Williams in Kingston, died 20 October 1805; her husband, born 1764, died 10 April 1830. [Kingston gravestone, Jamaica]

WILLIAM, GEORGE, born 1734, a peruke-maker from London, bound via London aboard the Royal Charlotte for Jamaica in 1774. [TNA.T47.9/11]

WILLIAMS, HENRY, an estate owner in Jamaica, married Miss Knight, daughter of James Knight in Stoke Newington on6 December 1739. [GM.9.666]

WILLIAMS, JOHN, born 1747, a seaman from Bristol, bound via Bristol for Jamaica in 1774. [TNA.T47.9/11]

WILLIAMS, JOHN, an estate owner in Jamaica, died in London on 9 December 1744. [GM.14.676]

WILLIAMS, SAMUEL, Secretary of Jamaica, died in May 1751. [GM.21.234]

WILLIAMS, THOMAS BULL, married Mary Sophia Forbes, daughter of John Forbes of New Providence, in Jamaica on 24 June 1820. [GM.90.636]; born 1788, from London, died at Orange Grove, Jamaica, on15 November 1840. [GM.ns15.558]

THE PEOPLE OF JAMAICA, 1655 TO 1855

WILLIAMS, MARTIN, a planter returning to Jamaica aboard the St James Planter via Portsmouth in 1775. [TNA.T47.9/11]

WILLIAMS, MAURICE, master of the Jamaica [formerly the Rabba Bispa] a privateer at Port Royal in 1659. [BM.Add.mss.12423]

WILLIAMS, PRISCILLA, died 1736. [Kingston gravestone, Jamaica]

WILLIAMS, THOMAS, in Jamaica, died 17 January 1762. [GM.32.135]

WILLIAMS, THOMAS B., from Jamaica, married Mary Sophia Forbes, from New Providence on 24 June 1820. [GM.90.636]

WILLIAMS, WILLIAM, died in Jamaica on 27 January 1749. [GM.19.92]

WILLIAMS, WILLIAM, born 1752, a merchant from Liverpool, bound aboard the Mary via Liverpool to Jamaica in 1774. [TNA.T47.9/11]

WILLIAMSON, MATHEW, born 1752, a carpenter from London, bound via London aboard the Royal Charlotte for Jamaica in 1774. [TNA.T47.9/11]

WILLIAMSON, Mrs, wife of Major General Williamson the Lieutenant Governor of Jamaica, died in King's House, Spanish Town, Jamaica, on 19 September 1794. [GM.64.1150]

WILLIS, Dr ADAM, died in Good Hope, Trelawney, Jamaica, on 15 October 1801. [GM.71,1211]

WILLIS, JAMES, from London, died in Jamaica in December 1793. [GM.64.180]

WILLISEY, JAMES, at Port Royal, Jamaica, 1817. [Liverpool Record Office, Tarleton papers. Kf152]

WILLS, GEORGE, late of Jamaica, probate, 1656, PCC

THE PEOPLE OF JAMAICA, 1655 TO 1855

WILSON, CATHERINE, born 1751, from London, bound via London aboard the Hope for Jamaica in 1774. [TNA.T47.9/11]

WILSON, HARRY, formerly of Lloyd's Coffee House, for many years in Jamaica, died in Spanish Town, Jamaica, on 20 March 1821. [GM.91.475]

WILSON, JOHN, died in Jamaica, admin., 1657, PCC

WILSON, JOHN, of Broomfield, deeds re property in St George's, Jamaica, 1751. [Sheffield Central Library, MD170]

WILSON, JOHN, Deputy Postmaster General of Jamaica, died in Kingston, Jamaica, on 2 July 1850. [GM.ns34.454]

WILSON, REGINALD, Naval Officer, died in the earthquake of 1692. [JHR.viii.60-62]

WILSON, ROBERT, a planter of 12 acres in St Andrew's parish, Jamaica, in 1754. [TNA.CO137/28/171-196]

WINCHESTER, WILLIAM, a planter of 500 acres in St Andrew's parish, Jamaica, in 1754. [TNA.CO137/28/171-196]

WINDE, SCUDAMORE, a judge and assemblyman in Jamaica, died 14 October 1775. [GM.45.607]

WINDER, THOMAS, born 1757, of St Anne's, Jamaica, died in London on 6 January 1816. [GM.86.184]

WINGAR, WILLIAM, a baker on Queen Street, Port Royal, 1684. [Jamaica Archives. Inventories.i]

WINTER, GEORGE, died in Jamaica on 29 July 1800. [GM.70.1004]

WYNTER, WILLIAM, a Councillor of Jamaica, died 1772. [GM.42.342]

WISE, THOMAS, born 1755, a surgeon returning to Jamaica via London aboard the Northampton in 1774. [TNA.T47.9/11]

THE PEOPLE OF JAMAICA, 1655 TO 1855

WOLFE, DAVID, a merchant in Kingston, Jamaica, a deed, 1819. [NRS.RD5.193.713]

WOLFE, ELLIS, a merchant in Kingston, Jamaica, reference in a deed. [NRS.RD5.193.713]

WOLFE, MARGARET, in Kingston, Jamaica, reference in a deed. [NRS.RD5.193.713]

WOOLFE, MAXIMILION, from Manchester, Jamaica, married Maria Cohen, daughter of Hyman Cohen, in London on 19 September 1821. [GM.91.372]

WOOD, CHARLES HENRY, born 1801, son of Reverend W. Wood in Grenton, Somerset, died in Longville, Jamaica, in 1820. [GM.90.476]

WOOD, MARGARET, born 1756, from London, via London aboard the Nancy bound for Jamaica in 1774. [TNA.T47.9/11]

WOOD, Dr ROBERT, a surgeon in Port Royal, Jamaica, died on 24 February 1795. [GM.65.439]

WOOD, THOMAS, died in Jamaica, admin., 1657, PCC

WOOD, WILLIAM, born 1714, a gentleman from Surrey, bound via London aboard the Royal Charlotte for Jamaica in 1774. [TNA.T47.9/11]

WOODCOCK, JAMES, married Miss Croft, daughter of Sir Arthur Croft in Barbados, in Jamaica in 1777. [GM.48.237]

WOODWARD, JOHN, from Stepney, London, died in Jamaica, administration, 1659, PCC

WOODWARD, JOHN, fought at the Battle of Sedgemoor in Somerset, on 6 July 1685 against the forces of King James II, captured and transported from Portland Road aboard the Jamaican Merchant of London, master Charles Gardiner, bound for Jamaica in 1685.

THE PEOPLE OF JAMAICA, 1655 TO 1855

WOOLFF, MAXIMILIAN, in Manchester, Jamaica, married Maria Cohen, in London on 19 September 1821. [GM.91.372]

WOOLVIN, PHILIP, of Jamaica, probate in February 1657. [PCC]

WRIGHT, ANDREW, born 1752, a millwright, with his wife Mary, born 1752, returning via London aboard the George Booth bound for Jamaica in 1774. [TNA.T47.9/11]

WRIGHT, HELEN FRANCES, daughter of W. Burt Wright in Jamaica, married Reverend George Hill Clifton, in Ripple, Worcestershire, in London on 16 August 1842. [GM.ns18.421]

WRIGHT, SAMUEL, died in Jamaica, admin., 1657, PCC

WYNN, ISAAC LASCELLES, born 1736, a Quaker, died at Montego Bay, Jamaica, on 4 April 1808. [GM.78.557]

YATMAN, THOMAS, born 1756, a gentleman returning to Jamaica via London aboard the William and Mary in 1774. [TNA.T47.9/11]

YATES, AUGUSTA, daughter of Reverend H. S. Yates in Henlow, Bedfordshire, married Reverend Hubert H., Isaacs in Hopeton, Jamaica, on 3 August 1859. [GM.ns.2/7.414]

YATS, THOMAS, died in Jamaica in 1739. [GM.5.335]

YDANA, ISAAC, probate, 1733, Jamaica. [BM.MS21,931]

YDANA, JOSEPH, probate, 1748, Jamaica. [BM.MS21,931]

YDANA, MOSES, probate, 1741, Jamaica. [BM.MS21,931]

YORKE, PHILIP, Chief Clerk of the Supreme Court in Jamaica, died on 8 January 1741. [GM.11.50]

YOUNG, GEORGINA, daughter of Reverend George Young in Spanish Town, Jamaica, died in London on 29 May 1865. [GM.ns2/19.123[

YOUNG, JAMES, a planter of 300 acres in St Andrew's parish, Jamaica, in 1754. [TNA.CO137/28/171-196]

www.ingramcontent.com/pod-product-compliance
Lightning Source LLC
Chambersburg PA
CBHW061739270326
41928CB00011B/2294